Luke

Back to the Bible Study Guides

Genesis: A God of Purpose, A People of Promise

Exodus: God's Plan, God's People

Judges: Ordinary People, Extraordinary God

Proverbs: The Pursuit of God's Wisdom

Daniel: Resolute Faith in a Hostile World

Ruth and Esther: Stories of God's Grace

John: Face-to-Face with Jesus

Ephesians: Life in God's Family

Philippians: Maturing in the Christian Life

1 & 2 Thessalonians: Trusting Until Christ Returns

Hebrews: Our Superior Savior

James: Living Your Faith

Revelation: The Glorified Christ

LUKE

GLORY TO GOD IN THE HIGHEST!

WOODROW KROLL

CROSSWAY BOOKS
WHEATON, ILLINOIS

Produced with the assistance of The Livingstone Corporation (www.LivingstoneCorp.com).

Project Staff: Neil Wilson

CH		19	18	17	16	15	14	13	12	11	10	09
15	14	13	12	11	10	9	8	7	6	5	4	3	2	1

Table of Contents

How to Use This Study

Selected passages of Luke from the ESV are printed before each day's devotional reading, so that everything you need is in one place. While we recommend reading the Scripture passage before you read the devotional, some have found it helpful to use the devotional as preparation for reading the Scripture. If you are unfamiliar with the English Standard Version (on which this series of studies is based), you might consider reading the included Bible selection, then the devotional, then the passage again from a version that is more familiar to you. This will give you an excellent biblical basis for considering the rest of the lesson.

After each devotional, there are three sections designed to help you better understand and apply the lesson's Scripture passage.

Consider It—Several questions will give you a better understanding of the Scripture passage of the day. These could be used for a small group discussion.

Express It—Suggestions to help you personalize insights from the lesson.

Go Deeper—Throughout this study, you will benefit from seeing how the Book of Luke fits with the rest of the Bible. This additional section will include other passages and insights from Scripture. The Go Deeper section will also allow you to consider some of the implications of the day's passage for the central theme of the study as well as other key Scripture themes.

If God Says . . .

Seemingly impossible obstacles allow God to prove He is an all-powerful God, the God of the impossible. What God says, He always does.

Read Luke 1:1–80
Luke 1:1–38

1 Inasmuch as many have undertaken to compile a narrative of the things that have been accomplished among us, [2]just as those who from the beginning were eyewitnesses and ministers of the word have delivered them to us, [3]it seemed good to me also, having followed all things closely for some time past, to write an orderly account for you, most excellent Theophilus, [4]that you may have certainty concerning the things you have been taught.

Key Verse

"For nothing will be impossible with God" (Luke 1:37).

Birth of John the Baptist Foretold

[5]In the days of Herod, king of Judea, there was a priest named Zechariah, of the division of Abijah. And he had a wife from the daughters of Aaron, and her name was Elizabeth. [6]And they were both righteous before God, walking blamelessly in all the commandments and statutes of the Lord. [7]But they had no child, because Elizabeth was barren, and both were advanced in years.

[8]Now while he was serving as priest before God when his division was on duty, [9]according to the custom of the priesthood, he was chosen by lot to enter the temple of the Lord and burn incense. [10]And the whole multitude of the people were praying outside at the hour of incense. [11]And there appeared to him an angel of the Lord standing on the right side of the altar of incense. [12]And Zechariah was troubled when he saw him, and fear fell upon him. [13]But the angel said to him, "Do not be afraid, Zechariah, for your prayer has been heard, and your wife Elizabeth will bear you a son, and you shall call his name John. [14]And you will have joy and gladness, and many will rejoice at his birth, [15]for he will be great before the Lord. And he must not drink wine or strong drink, and he will be filled with the Holy Spirit, even from his mother's

[18]And Zechariah said to the angel, "How shall I know this? For I am an old man, and my wife is advanced in years." [19]And the angel answered him, "I am Gabriel. I stand in the presence of God, and I was sent to speak to you and to bring you this good news. [20]And behold, you will be silent and unable to speak until the day that these things take place, because you did not believe my words, which will be fulfilled in their time." [21]And the people were waiting for Zechariah, and they were wondering at his delay in the temple. [22]And when he came out, he was unable to speak to them, and they realized that he had seen a vision in the temple. And he kept making signs to them and remained mute. [23]And when his time of service was ended, he went to his home.

[24]After these days his wife Elizabeth conceived, and for five months she kept herself hidden, saying, [25]"Thus the Lord has done for me in the days when he looked on me, to take away my reproach among people."

Birth of Jesus Foretold

[26]In the sixth month the angel Gabriel was sent from God to a city of Galilee named Nazareth, [27]to a virgin betrothed to a man whose name was Joseph, of the house of David. And the virgin's name

was Mary. [28]And he came to her and said, "Greetings, O favored one, the Lord is with you!" [29]But she was greatly troubled at the saying, and tried to discern what sort of greeting this might be. [30]And the angel said to her, "Do not be afraid, Mary, for you have found favor with God. [31]And behold, you will conceive in your womb and bear a son, and you shall call his name Jesus. [32]He will be great and will be called the Son of the Most High. And the Lord God will give to him the throne of his father David, [33]and he will reign over the house of Jacob forever, and of his kingdom there will be no end."

[34]And Mary said to the angel, "How will this be, since I am a virgin?"

[35]And the angel answered her, "The Holy Spirit will come upon you, and the power of the Most High will overshadow you; therefore the child to be born will be called holy—the Son of God. [36]And behold, your relative Elizabeth in her old age has also conceived a son, and this is the sixth month with her who was called barren. [37]For nothing will be impossible with God." [38]And Mary said, "Behold, I am the servant of the Lord; let it be to me according to your word." And the angel departed from her.

A n old saying claims: "If something is too good to be true, it probably isn't." Perhaps a similar thought was in Zechariah's mind the day he got a message from an angel of the Lord.

Zechariah and his wife, Elizabeth, were "righteous before God, walking blamelessly in all the commandments" (Luke 1:6). But both were also "advanced in years," and they had no children (v. 7). This elderly couple lived in the hill country of Judea. But when we first meet Zechariah, he is in Jerusalem because he was a priest, and it was his turn to serve in the temple. To be a priest Zechariah had to be descended from Jacob's son, Levi. In fact, he also had to be a direct descendant of a specific son of Levi—Aaron, who was the brother of Moses and the first priest appointed by God (Ex. 28:1).

The priests were divided into 24 groups or divisions of 50 each. Zechariah was a priest of the division of Abijah. Each week a new group would assume their duties in the temple. And each day one of them would be chosen by lot to enter the second most sacred place in

> *"Faith is not a mindless leap into the dark. We don't need signs and wonders to engender faith; we just need a thorough knowledge of what God has said in His Word."*

the temple, the Holy Place, to burn incense at the time of the morning and evening sacrifice. (The Holy Place, located just outside the Holy of Holies [the most holy place in the temple], contained three items considered extremely sacred to the Israelites: a lampstand, a table with 12 loaves of bread and an altar for burning incense.)

One day the lot fell to Zechariah. As the people prayed outside, "May the merciful God enter the Holy Place and accept with favor the offering of his people," Zechariah entered the Holy Place to burn the incense on the altar. Can you imagine his excitement to have such a great privilege?

But that was nothing compared to what happened next. As he was going about his duties in the Holy Place, suddenly an angel of the Lord appeared at the right side of the altar of incense. From that moment on, Zechariah's life was never the same.

"The angel said to him, 'Do not be afraid, Zechariah, for your prayer has been heard, and your wife Elizabeth will bear you a son'" (Luke 1:13). The heavenly messenger then went on to inform Zechariah that the mission of this child would be to turn the hearts of the people back to God and prepare the way for the Lord.

To say that Zechariah was stunned would probably be an understatement. Flabbergasted might be more like it. "'How shall I know this?'" Zechariah responded. It didn't take a degree in biology to realize that he and Elizabeth were well beyond the standard age to conceive and bear a child.

The angel's response was both a sign and a punishment. The angel answered him and said, "I am Gabriel. I stand in the presence of God, and I was sent to speak to you and to bring you this good news. And behold, you will be silent and unable to speak until the day that these things take place, because you did not believe my words, which will be fulfilled in their time" (vv. 19–20).

Fast forward six months and the same angel appeared to a young Jewish maiden, Mary, with another startling announcement, "Behold, you will conceive in your womb and bear a son, and you shall call His name Jesus" (v. 31).

Mary replied, "How will this be, since I am a virgin?" How was Mary's response different from Zechariah's? Why was Zechariah punished for his question while Mary's question was permitted? As a priest, Zechariah knew his Bible thoroughly. He certainly would have been familiar with the Old Testament story of Abraham and Sarah, another couple who conceived a child in their old age. So, he should have known that Gabriel was speaking the truth. On the other hand, in Mary's defense, no one ever before and no one ever again will conceive a child apart from a human father.

God is always ready to prove the impossible. Faith is not a mindless leap into the dark. Romans 10:17 says, "So faith comes from hearing, and hearing through the word of Christ." God has given us the Bible to be the basis for our faith. We don't need signs and wonders to engender faith; we just need a thorough knowledge of what God has said in His Word.

Make sure you take time to read and study your Bible. It's through His Word that God reveals His glorious character. That's where we discover that He is the God of the impossible. Impossible for an elderly couple to conceive? Impossible for a virgin to bring forth a child? Not with God. Jeremiah 32:27 says, "Behold, I am the LORD, the God of all flesh. Is anything too hard for me?"

Rejoice today that you have a God who is not stumped by the impossible. It's all part of His glory.

Go Deeper

God gave His final Old Testament revelation to the prophet Malachi, saying: "Behold, I will send you Elijah the prophet before the great and awesome day of the LORD comes" (Mal. 4:5). By the time John the Baptist was born, God had not spoken to His Chosen People, Israel, for four hundred years. That's a long time! It's almost twice as long as the United States has been a nation. During that time Israel was under the influence of Persia, Greece, and finally, Rome. Jewish religious groups such as the Pharisees, Sadducees, and Essenes were formed in the years between the Old and New Testaments. The scribes became the official interpreters of Jewish Law. But from the Living God came nothing but silence.

Jesus told His disciples that John the Baptist fulfilled Malachi's prophecy (Matt. 17:10–13). He was the forerunner and herald of the Savior (Mark 1:3,7–8). Like Jesus, John was rejected and killed (Mark 6:14–29), but the impact of his ministry lasted long after his death. All four Gospels refer to him. Without John, Israel would have been even less prepared for the Messiah's coming.

At Jesus' birth, shepherds were astounded by the angels' words: "Glory to God in the highest" (Luke 2:14). But it was John the Baptist who years later had both the privilege and responsibility of introducing this "Glory of God" to the people (Luke 3:15–22).

Express It

Thank God that He is the God of the impossible. If you have a situation that seems impossible, tell God about it. Let Him know that you believe He is able to accomplish all things because of what He did in the lives of Elizabeth and Zechariah and in the lives of Mary and Joseph.

Then look back at your own past problems. Were there difficulties that looked, at the time, like no solution would ever be found? Remind yourself how God worked those problems out by making a chart with dates and solutions noted.

Consider It

As you read Luke 1:1–80, consider these questions:

1) What is Luke's goal in writing this Gospel?

2) What kind of people were Zechariah and Elizabeth?

3) What do these verses tell us about the angel who visited Zechariah?

4) How did the angel describe the son whom God promised to Zechariah and Elizabeth?

5) Whose spirit and power was to characterize the child?

6) How did Elizabeth respond to the startling news?

7) How do you respond when God answers a long-requested prayer?

Glory to God

God's glory is not a "something," it's a Someone. His Son came to live in our midst and show us the true glory of God. And it all began in a stable in an insignificant little town called Bethlehem.

Read Luke 2:1–52

Luke 2:1–38

The Birth of Jesus Christ

2 In those days a decree went out from Caesar Augustus that all the world should be registered. ²This was the first registration when Quirinius was governor of Syria. ³And all went to be registered, each to his own town. ⁴And Joseph also went up from Galilee, from the town of Nazareth, to Judea, to the city of David, which is called Bethlehem, because he was of the house and lineage of David, ⁵to be registered with Mary, his betrothed, who was with child. ⁶And while they were there, the time came for her to give birth. ⁷And she gave birth to her firstborn son and wrapped him in swaddling cloths and laid him in a manger, because there was no place for them in the inn.

The Shepherds and the Angels

⁸And in the same region there were shepherds out in the field, keeping watch over their flock by night. ⁹And an angel of the Lord appeared to them, and the glory of the Lord shone around them, and they were filled with fear. ¹⁰And the angel said to them, "Fear not, for behold, I bring you good news of great joy that will be for all the people. ¹¹For unto you is born this day in the city of David a Savior, who is Christ the Lord. ¹²And this will be a sign for you: you will find a baby wrapped in swaddling cloths and lying in a manger." ¹³And suddenly there was with the angel a multitude of the heavenly host praising God and saying,

¹⁴"Glory to God in the highest,
and on earth peace among those with whom he is pleased!"

¹⁵When the angels went away from them into heaven, the shepherds said to one another, "Let us go over to Bethlehem and see this thing that has

> # Key Verse
>
> *And while they were there, the time came for her to give birth. And she gave birth to her firstborn son and wrapped him in swaddling cloths and laid him in a manger, because there was no place for them in the inn* (Luke 2:6–7).

which the Lord has made known to us." ¹⁶And they went with haste and found Mary and Joseph, and the baby lying in a manger. ¹⁷And when they saw it, they made known the saying that had been told them concerning this child. ¹⁸And all who heard it wondered at what the shepherds told them. ¹⁹But Mary treasured up all these things, pondering them in her heart. ²⁰And the shepherds returned, glorifying and praising God for all they had heard and seen, as it had been told them.

²¹And at the end of eight days, when he was circumcised, he was called Jesus, the name given by the angel before he was conceived in the womb.

Jesus Presented at the Temple

²²And when the time came for their purification according to the Law of Moses, they brought him up to Jerusalem to present him to the Lord ²³(as it is written in the Law of the Lord, "Every male who first opens the womb shall be called holy to the Lord") ²⁴and to offer a

sacrifice according to what is said in the Law of the Lord, "a pair of turtledoves, or two young pigeons." 25Now there was a man in Jerusalem, whose name was Simeon, and this man was righteous and devout, waiting for the consolation of Israel, and the Holy Spirit was upon him. 26And it had been revealed to him by the Holy Spirit that he would not see death before he had seen the Lord's Christ. 27And he came in the Spirit into the temple, and when the parents brought in the child Jesus, to do for him according to the custom of the Law, 28he took him up in his arms and blessed God and said,

29"Lord, now you are letting your servant depart in peace, according to your word;

30 for my eyes have seen your salvation

31 that you have prepared in the presence of all peoples,

32 a light for revelation to the Gentiles, and for glory to your people Israel."

33And his father and his mother marveled at what was said about him. 34And Simeon blessed them and said to Mary his mother, "Behold, this child is appointed for the fall and rising of many in Israel, and for a sign that is opposed 35(and a sword will pierce through your own soul also), so that thoughts from many hearts may be revealed."

36And there was a prophetess, Anna, the daughter of Phanuel, of the tribe of Asher. She was advanced in years, having lived with her husband seven years from when she was a virgin, 37and then as a widow until she was eighty-four. She did not depart from the temple, worshiping with fasting and prayer night and day. 38And coming up at that very hour she began to give thanks to God and to speak of him to all who were waiting for the redemption of Jerusalem.

The opening years of the 19th century were dark. Napoleon was ruthlessly pushing his way through Europe. Everywhere there was talk of invasion, war, and bloodshed. The power-hungry French dictator extended his control over one country after another, spreading despair and hopelessness as he advanced across the continent.

In 1809 Napoleon was in the process of subduing Austria. In England, people were occupied with news of Napoleon's troop advances and the outcome of sieges and battles. Most paid little attention when the Gladstone family welcomed the arrival of little William, destined to become one of the greatest statesmen England ever produced. Equally obscure was the birth of Alfred Lord Tennyson to an unheard-of minister and his wife. During that same year Oliver

"The troubles of our world seem overwhelming. Wars, natural disasters, the economy—these are the things that capture the headlines. Yet these things are barely blips on the radar of eternity."

Wendell Holmes was born in Cambridge, Massachusetts, and Charles Robert Darwin in Shrewsbury, England. And, not to be forgotten, in a small log cabin in Hardin County, Kentucky, the Lincoln family welcomed a baby boy whom they named Abraham.

It was not the battles of that year that were destined to change the world; it was the babies. Babies do that when they become adults. But another baby born long before 1809 had an even greater impact than any of these 1809 babies: He was Mary's firstborn son, Jesus. He was born at a dark time. The Roman Empire had extended its iron grip over most of the known world. The Empire boasted a population of 45 million and covered, at its peak, nearly 2.2 million square miles. It was an empire that had no equal. The Romans crushed any rebellion that dared raise its head and placed every conquered country under heavy taxation.

Judea was one of those countries. In 61 B.C., the Roman general, Pompey, conquered the Jewish nation, overran Jerusalem, and defiled the Jewish temple. (Israel never became an independent country again until 1947.)

It was into this culture Jesus was born. As the Jewish people struggled under the unreasonable demands of a Roman demagogue, Caesar Augustus, most were too caught up in the troubles of the day to notice or care about a baby born in a Bethlehem stable. Only a handful of shepherds watching their flocks in the nearby fields were given the blessed opportunity to greet the Savior of the world at His birth. Just two elderly servants of God, Anna and Simeon, recognized the Messiah when He was later brought to the temple. But this lack of attention could not diminish the fact that God's glory had been born into the world in human form.

And what a birth it was! Promised as far back as the days of Adam and Eve (Gen. 3:15), foretold by prophets, priests, and kings, it reached its climactic conclusion in the smelly stable of an unknown innkeeper located in the tiny backwater village of Bethlehem. As the apostle Paul noted, "But when the fullness of time had come, God sent forth his Son, born of woman, born under the law, to redeem those who were under the law, so that we might receive adoption as sons" (Gal. 4:4–5). Jesus' birth was heralded by the highest angels in heaven but, for the most part, was ignored by the people whom He came to save. His birth was overshadowed by the decrees of a Roman dictator, yet this baby was destined to change the world in ways this dictator couldn't imagine.

And so it goes even today. The troubles of our world seem overwhelming. Wars, natural disasters, the economy—these are the things that capture the headlines. Yet these things are barely blips on the radar of eternity. What will still be relevant a million years from now, a trillion years from now, is the glory of God swaddled in the body of a baby in Bethlehem.

Be careful that the earthly trials you face don't cause you to miss the eternal glory of God. Jesus said, "In the world you will have tribulation." Not "you might have" or "you could have," but "you will have" tribulation. It's a given. But don't be discouraged. Jesus goes on to say, "But take heart; I have overcome the world" (John 16:33).

The message of the angels to the shepherds was, "Glory to God in the highest, and on earth peace among those with whom he is pleased!" (Luke 2:14). Your situation may be disheartening, it may be sad, it may even be painful; but keep Jesus as your focus. Jesus has overcome the world, including your present situation. In Him you can find peace in the midst of your difficulties.

Go Deeper

Luke 2:1 makes it clear that God is in charge. Had God not been moving in human affairs, Jesus would have been born in Nazareth of Galilee, Joseph's hometown. God, however, had promised Jesus' birth nearly seven hundred years before through the prophet Micah:

"But you, O Bethlehem Ephrathah, who are too little to be among the clans of Judah, from you shall come forth for me one who is to be ruler in Israel, whose coming forth is from of old, from ancient days" (Micah 5:2).

God's plan for the Messiah's birth was this: It would happen in King David's hometown, Bethlehem. Caesar Augustus, ruler of the vast Roman Empire that included Israel, knew nothing of such a prophecy. He had only an empire-wide taxation plan in mind, but that meant Joseph and Mary were compelled to go to Bethlehem, where the King of the Jews and Savior of the world was destined to arrive. God used Caesar's greed to accomplish His divine purposes. However, Jewish scholars of Jesus' day knew Micah's prophecy well, as did many of the common people. (See Matt. 2:1–6 and John 7:40–42.)

This should encourage every believer to glorify God for His infallible Word. When God says it, the whole world is His instrument to make sure it happens.

Express It

Does the constant barrage of news, the differing political voices, and the disaster-predicting "talk" shows cause you to concentrate on the urgencies of this world? This week, make a concerted effort to take a few moments on at least four different days to focus on Jesus. On these days, turn off the radio or TV and read your Bible for at least ten minutes. Pray and ask God to allow you to see those He's placed in your life through His eyes. Spend some time on these days listening to Christian music. And then do one thing that will purposely impact a life for eternity—write a note to someone who needs encouragement, read a story about Jesus to a child, or do something special for a new family at church.

Consider It

As you read Luke 2:1–52, consider these questions:

1) **What does this event tell you about God's timing? His sovereignty?**

_____

_____

_____

2) **What do these verses tell you about Joseph and Mary?**

_____

_____

_____

3) **What is the "good news of great joy" really about?**

_____

_____

_____

4) **How did this affect the shepherds?**

_____

_____

_____

5) **How has this news affected your life?**

_____

_____

_____

6) **What did Simeon and Anna have in common?**

_____

_____

_____

7) **What can you take from the example of Simeon and Anna as you get older?**

_____

_____

_____

Lesson

3

A Voice Crying in the Wilderness

It's one thing to claim repentance; it's another to live it. John's message was to not only repent, but to change the way you live to reflect that repentance.

Read Luke 3:1–38

Luke 3:1–22

John the Baptist Prepares the Way

3 In the fifteenth year of the reign of Tiberius Caesar, Pontius Pilate being governor of Judea, and Herod being tetrarch of Galilee, and his brother Philip tetrarch of the region of Ituraea and Trachonitis, and Lysanias tetrarch of Abilene, ²during the high priesthood of Annas and Caiaphas, the word of God came to John the son of Zechariah in the wilderness. ³And he went into all the region around the Jordan, proclaiming a baptism of repentance for the forgiveness of sins. ⁴As it is written in the book of the words of Isaiah the prophet,

> "The voice of one crying in the wilderness: 'Prepare the way of the Lord, make his paths straight.
>
> ⁵ Every valley shall be filled, and every mountain and hill shall be made low, and the crooked shall become straight, and the rough places shall become level ways,
>
> ⁶ and all flesh shall see the salvation of God.'"

⁷He said therefore to the crowds that came out to be baptized by him, "You brood of vipers! Who warned you to flee from the wrath to come? ⁸Bear fruits in keeping with repentance. And do not begin to say to yourselves, 'We have Abraham as our father.' For I tell you, God is able from these stones to raise up children for Abraham. ⁹Even now the axe is laid to the root of the trees. Every tree therefore that does not bear good fruit is cut down and thrown into the fire."

¹⁰And the crowds asked him, "What then shall we do?" ¹¹And he answered them, "Whoever has two tunics is to share with him who has none, and whoever has food is to do likewise." ¹²Tax collectors also came to be baptized and said to him, "Teacher, what shall we do?" ¹³And he said to them, "Collect no more than you are authorized to do." ¹⁴Soldiers also asked him, "And we, what shall we do?" And he said to them, "Do not extort money from anyone by threats or by false accusation, and be content with your wages."

¹⁵As the people were in expectation, and all were questioning in their hearts concerning John, whether he might be the Christ, ¹⁶John answered them all, saying, "I baptize you with water, but he who is mightier than I is coming, the strap of whose sandals I am not worthy to untie. He will baptize you with the Holy Spirit and with fire. ¹⁷His winnowing fork is in his hand, to clear his threshing floor and to gather the wheat into his barn, but the chaff he will burn with unquenchable fire."

¹⁸So with many other exhortations he preached good news to the people. ¹⁹But Herod the tetrarch, who had been reproved by him for Herodias, his brother's wife, and for all the evil things that Herod had done, ²⁰added this to them all, that he locked up John in prison.

Key Verse

"Bear fruits in keeping with repentance. And do not begin to say to yourselves, 'We have Abraham as our father.' For I tell you, God is able from these stones to raise up children for Abraham" (Luke 3:8).

²¹Now when all the people were baptized, and when Jesus also had been baptized and was praying, the heavens were opened, ²²and the Holy Spirit descended on him in bodily form, like a dove; and a voice came from heaven, "You are my beloved Son; with you I am well pleased."

The time: around A.D. 28/29. The political scene: turmoil, both in Rome and in Judea. Into this hotbed of political intrigue and unrest came a man who could only have been called "unusual." Dressed in camel hair and living off a diet of locusts and honey, John the Baptist broke onto the scene like a thunderstorm in May.

God had not sent a prophet to His people since the days of Malachi—four hundred years earlier. But that was about to change. John the Baptist's powerful preaching drew crowds from all Israel. He was known at every level of Jewish society. (See Luke 3:10–14.) His message of repentance and God's coming kingdom pierced the conscience of a nation that had drifted far from God.

John laid it on the line. The people needed to turn from their sins and get ready because the Messiah whom God promised was at the door. And this turning (or repentance) required more than mouthing words; it was to bear the fruits of repentance—namely, a changed life.

You can be sure his condemnation of the Pharisees and Sadducees as a "brood of vipers" didn't set well with these self-

> *"Our day-to-day fellowship with God is affected by the sins that litter our pathway. How cluttered is your pathway? Have you cleared it up through repentance and confession or do you still have obstacles in the way of your relationship with the Lord?"*

righteous people (Matt. 3:7). They thought they could claim special treatment because they traced their ancestors back to Abraham. Yet John warned them that genealogies and pedigrees didn't impress God. Godly living was what He required.

But the common people took John's teachings to heart. The crowds cried out, "What then shall we do?" (Luke 3:10). And John's directions were to share what they had with those who needed it. Even the tax collectors, hired hands of the Roman government and despised by their fellow Jews, were convicted by John's preaching and asked, "Teacher, what shall we do?" John's reply went right to the heart of the matter: "Collect no more than you are authorized to do." Since tax collectors were allowed to keep whatever they could squeeze out of the people over and above the legitimate taxes they owed, this was hitting them in their pocketbook, a blow that was sure to hurt.

And then there were the soldiers. In all likelihood these were Jewish soldiers hired to guard the temple or part of a personal bodyguard for the Jewish nobility. God had a message for them too: "Do not extort money from anyone by threats or by false accusation, and be content with your wages." Like most soldiers, they probably were not paid very well, and the temptation must have been great to simply take what they wanted.

God always gets to the heart of the matter—and, invariably, the heart of the matter is sin. Repentance meant a turning away from these things and a turning toward God. The "baptism of repentance" John offered was a symbol that the person being baptized had turned from his or her sins and was beginning a new life.

After Jesus began His ministry, Herod Antipas imprisoned John (Matt. 14:3–5) because the courageous prophet confronted him and his wife, Herodias, over their sinful relationship. While in prison in a moment of uncertainty, John sent some messengers to ask Jesus if He was indeed the Messiah. Jesus quoted Isaiah 61:1, which prophesied His ministry (Luke 7:22–23). His answer put to rest any doubts, but John never got to see the ultimate outcome of Jesus' ministry. Herod beheaded the prophet as a favor to Herodias' daughter (Matt. 14:6–12).

John declared the purpose of his ministry was to "prepare the way of the Lord" (Luke 3:4). This meant clearing the path of any obstacle that would hinder the Lord's way. And sin is always such a hindrance. The religious people struggled with pride. The common people had to deal with selfishness. The tax collectors were tempted by greed. The soldiers had to resist the abuse of power and authority. What do you need to face up to? What needs to be cleared from your life to prepare the way of the Lord?

While our salvation is based on what Christ did on the cross, our day-to-day fellowship with God is affected by the sins that litter our pathway. The solution is to confess and turn from these sins. "If we confess our sins, he is faithful and just to forgive us our sins and to cleanse us from all unrighteousness" (1 John 1:9).

How cluttered is your pathway? Have you cleared it up through repentance and confession or do you still have obstacles in the way of your relationship with the Lord? If you don't know Christ as your Savior, surrender your life to Him now. If you have strayed from that relationship, now is the time to turn from your sins and begin again a life of fellowship with God.

Go Deeper

God not only picks His places, He also picks His times. And the time could not have been more opportune for the ministry of John the Baptist and, later, Jesus. When times are uncertain, people are open to the things of God. And in the time of John and Jesus, the political scene was very uncertain.

Tiberius Caesar was on the throne in Rome. Unlike his stepfather, Caesar Augustus, Tiberius was a very unpopular ruler. Eventually he was assassinated.

In Israel, Herod Antipas, the son of Herod the Great who ruled when Jesus was born, was tetrarch of Galilee. A tetrarch was a ruler or governor under the authority of the Roman government. Literally, it meant a "ruler of fourths." As an Idumean (someone from Edom in southern Jordan), Herod Antipas was no better liked than his father.

Herod Antipas's half brother, Philip (also called Herod Philip), was tetrarch in the region of Ituraea and Trachonitis. It was Philip's wife, Herodias, who created even more bad blood between the Herodian family and the Jewish people by divorcing Philip and marrying Herod Antipas.

In Judea, Herod Archelaus, another son of Herod the Great, proved to be an incompetent ruler and thus was replaced by Pontius Pilate.

When people cannot find security in the world around them, they look for security in God. John announced it; Jesus secured it. God's kingdom was at hand.

Express It

What temptations do you struggle with? Men and women often battle different kinds of temptation. Studies show that men struggle most often with sexual temptations, while ladies don't appear to have a "most often" category. They fight a lot of different temptations: gossip, overeating, spending too much, etc.

Whatever the temptations you face, God can help you be victorious. Write out a scripture that will help you fight whatever temptation plagues you. (Try 1 Cor. 10:13 or James 1:12.) Put this verse in your pocket or purse and look at it when you need strength to overcome temptation.

Consider It

As you read Luke 3:1–38, consider these questions:

1) What was the core of John the Baptist's message?

_____

_____

_____

2) Make a list of the groups of people who came to hear John. What was each group's response to his message?

_____

_____

_____

3) What social issues did John address and how?

_____

_____

_____

4) How did John answer those who thought he was the Messiah?

_____

_____

_____

5) Write down the three things that happened when Jesus was baptized.

_____

_____

_____

6) Speaking up for God isn't popular; what happened to John when he did?

_____

_____

_____

7) How do you speak up for God today?

_____

_____

_____

Trust and Obey

Isn't it strange that the religious leaders, who should have recognized Jesus the quickest, were the most reluctant to acknowledge who He was? Maybe it was because, once they admitted He was the Son of God, they would be faced with the necessity of obeying Him. That was something the scribes and the Pharisees had no intention of doing. What about you?

Luke 4:1–44

The Temptation of Jesus

4 And Jesus, full of the Holy Spirit, returned from the Jordan and was led by the Spirit in the wilderness ²for forty days, being tempted by the devil. And he ate nothing during those days. And when they were ended, he was hungry. ³The devil said to him, "If you are the Son of God, command this stone to become bread." ⁴And Jesus answered him, "It is written, 'Man shall not live by bread alone.'" ⁵And the devil took him up and showed him all the kingdoms of the world in a moment of time, ⁶and said to him, "To you I will give all this authority and their glory, for it has been delivered to me, and I give it to whom I will. ⁷If you, then, will worship me, it will all be yours." ⁸And Jesus answered him, "It is written,

> "'You shall worship the Lord your God, and him only shall you serve.'"

⁹And he took him to Jerusalem and set him on the pinnacle of the temple and said to him, "If you are the Son of God, throw yourself down from here, ¹⁰for it is written,

> "'He will command his angels concerning you, to guard you,'

¹¹and

> "'On their hands they will bear you up, lest you strike your foot against a stone.'"

¹²And Jesus answered him, "It is said, 'You shall not put the Lord your God to the test.'" ¹³And when the devil had ended every temptation, he departed from him until an opportune time.

Jesus Begins His Ministry

¹⁴And Jesus returned in the power of the Spirit to Galilee, and a report about

---

> # Key Verse
>
> *And they were all amazed and said to one another, "What is this word? For with authority and power he commands the unclean spirits, and they come out!"* (Luke 4:36).

---

went out through all the surrounding country. ¹⁵And he taught in their synagogues, being glorified by all.

Jesus Rejected at Nazareth

¹⁶And he came to Nazareth, where he had been brought up. And as was his custom, he went to the synagogue on the Sabbath day, and he stood up to read. ¹⁷And the scroll of the prophet Isaiah was given to him. He unrolled the scroll and found the place where it was written,

¹⁸"The Spirit of the Lord is upon me, because he has anointed me to proclaim good news to the poor. He has sent me to proclaim liberty to the captives and recovering of sight to the blind, to set at liberty those who are oppressed,

¹⁹ to proclaim the year of the Lord's favor."

²⁰And he rolled up the scroll and gave it back to the attendant and sat down. And the eyes of all in the synagogue were fixed on him. ²¹And he began to say to them, "Today this Scripture has been fulfilled in your hearing." ²²And all

spoke well of him and marveled at the gracious words that were coming from his mouth. And they said, "Is not this Joseph's son?" 23And he said to them, "Doubtless you will quote to me this proverb, 'Physician, heal yourself.' What we have heard you did at Capernaum, do here in your hometown as well." 24And he said, "Truly, I say to you, no prophet is acceptable in his hometown. 25But in truth, I tell you, there were many widows in Israel in the days of Elijah, when the heavens were shut up three years and six months, and a great famine came over all the land, 26and Elijah was sent to none of them but only to Zarephath, in the land of Sidon, to a woman who was a widow. 27And there were many lepers in Israel in the time of the prophet Elisha, and none of them was cleansed, but only Naaman the Syrian." 28When they heard these things, all in the synagogue were filled with wrath. 29And they rose up and drove him out of the town and brought him to the brow of the hill on which their town was built, so that they could throw him down the cliff. 30But passing through their midst, he went away.

Jesus Heals a Man with an Unclean Demon

31And he went down to Capernaum, a city of Galilee. And he was teaching them on the Sabbath, 32and they were astonished at his teaching, for his word possessed authority. 33And in the synagogue there was a man who had the spirit of an unclean demon, and he cried out with a loud voice, 34"Ha! What have you to do with us, Jesus of Nazareth? Have you come to destroy us? I know who you are—the Holy One of God." 35But Jesus rebuked him, saying, "Be silent and come out of him!" And when the demon had thrown him down in their midst, he came out of him, having done him no harm. 36And they were all amazed and said to one another, "What is this word? For with authority and power he commands the unclean spirits, and they come out!" 37And reports about him went out into every place in the surrounding region.

Jesus Heals Many

38And he arose and left the synagogue and entered Simon's house. Now Simon's mother-in-law was ill with a high fever, and they appealed to him on her behalf. 39And he stood over her and rebuked the fever, and it left her, and immediately she rose and began to serve them.

40Now when the sun was setting, all those who had any who were sick with various diseases brought them to him, and he laid his hands on every one of them and healed them. 41And demons also came out of many, crying, "You are the Son of God!" But he rebuked them and would not allow them to speak, because they knew that he was the Christ.

Jesus Preaches in Synagogues

42And when it was day, he departed and went into a desolate place. And the people sought him and came to him, and would have kept him from leaving them, 43but he said to them, "I must preach the good news of the kingdom of God to the other towns as well; for I was sent for this purpose." 44And he was preaching in the synagogues of Judea.

Many people are curious about Jesus' years as a child and a teenager. For the most part, Scripture is silent. Luke gives us a brief glimpse of Jesus as a boy of 12 (Luke 2:41–52) but nothing more. Imaginary tales of Jesus astounding his boyhood friends with miracles abound, but these have no basis in reality. Jesus never did miracles just for the amazement and amusement of the crowds.

But while Jesus' childhood and adolescence are shrouded in secrecy, His life from the age of 30 and on is known to the world. It was at this age Jesus first appeared to the public eye—and, of all places, it was at a baptismal service. John the Baptist had come administering a baptism of repentance. John called for people to turn away from their old lives of sin and begin a new life dedicated to doing what would please God. But Jesus had no sin (2 Cor. 5:21). Why then was He baptized? Perhaps Jesus' baptism announced He was turning from His old life as a carpenter and beginning a new life that was to bring glory to God. For a brief three years Jesus would reveal God's true character, His Father's glory, to the people around Him.

It's not strange, then, the first encounter after His baptism was with Satan in the wilderness (Luke 4:1–13). After all, Satan has been in the business of slandering God's character from the beginning. It was Satan who accused God of lying (Gen. 3:4). It was Satan who convinced Eve that God was not to be trusted (Gen. 3:5). And Satan tried these same tactics on Jesus, but they didn't work.

While Satan used Scripture, Jesus knew Scripture. He not only knew what the words said, He knew the character of the person who stood behind the words—God the Father. The appeal to the lust of the eyes, the lust of the flesh, and the pride of life (1 John 2:16) that seduced Eve was ineffective with Jesus. He chose to trust the glory of God rather than the lies of Satan.

Faced with defeat, Satan departed from Jesus "until an opportune time" (Luke 4:13). And that opportune time was not long in coming. When Jesus returned from His 40 days of fasting in the wilderness, it wasn't long before He ran into problems with the religious people in His hometown of Nazareth. Religion usually has its own ideas about

"The more we obey Jesus, the more we begin to look like Him. The more we look like Jesus, the more we reflect God's character. The more we reflect God's character, the greater we experience His glory."

what God is like. Jesus burst that bubble when He pointed out that in the days of Elijah and Elisha, God had passed up His own people and reached out to Gentiles like the widow of Sidon and Naaman the Syrian. How would you feel if someone told you that God had let Christians perish while He rescued some idol worshippers in a foreign country? Well, the religious people of Jesus' day were "filled with wrath" (v. 28). In fact, they drove Him out of town and were going to throw Him over a cliff, but He passed safely through their midst and out of their sight.

The apostle John declared, "He came to his own, and his own people did not receive him" (John 1:11). Even the demons recognized Jesus more quickly than the ones among whom He lived. When Jesus was driven out of Nazareth, He went to Capernaum, a town on the shores of the Sea of Galilee. It was there He cast a demon out of a man. When Jesus confronted this fallen creature, it confessed, "I know who you are—the Holy One of God" (Luke 4:34).

As Jesus continued into the evening healing and casting out demons from the crowds that flocked to Him, the unclean spirits frequently identified Him as "the Son of God" (vv. 40–41).

The demons knew Jesus and reluctantly obeyed Him. But obedience is doing what we're told to do, when we're told to do it, with the right heart attitude. If we truly know Jesus, we will obey Him without reluctance. When God has to drag obedience out of us, that's called disobedience. God's plan is for each of us to be "conformed to the image of His Son" (Rom. 8:29). The more we obey Jesus, the more we begin to look like Him. The more we look like Jesus, the more we reflect God's character. The more we reflect God's character, the greater we experience His glory.

As it has been said, "To become a Christian is easy; to live like one is another matter. We become Christians by repentance and faith; we live as Christians only to the extent that we obey Christ's commands." Jesus said, "Whoever has my commandments and keeps them, he it is who loves me. And he who loves me will be loved by my Father, and I will love him and manifest myself to him" (John 14:21). Make obedience that is done quickly and without complaining a priority in your life today.

Go Deeper

Luke, the "beloved physician" (Col. 4:14), was not alone in recognizing the difference between sickness and demon possession. (See Matt. 4:24; Mark 1:32–34; Acts 5:16.) In all these passages, diseases and evil spirits are distinguished.

Demon possession is real, although it's not easily recognizable in our day. The number of demons is limited and their activities apparently change according to the culture where they are carrying out Satan's program. The large number of cases of demon possession during Jesus' earthly ministry was because of Satan's all-out attack on the Son of God and God's plan of salvation. Satan's desire to foil Christ's work is clearly seen in the temptation of Jesus (Luke 4:1–13).

Few foreign missionaries doubt the reality of demons and their activity in people's lives today. It seems likely that we will see more of their activity as we approach the time of Christ's return.

But can demons possess a Christian believer? First John 4:4 says, "Little children, you are from God and have overcome them, for he [the Holy Spirit] who is in you is greater than he [Satan and his demons] who is in the world." This would mean that a demon could not overpower the Holy Spirit in us. And you can be sure the Spirit would not be willing to share His house (our bodies) with an unclean demon. Therefore we can be certain that while demons may attack God's children, demon possession for a Christian is not possible.

Express It

Obedience is important for the follower of Christ. Remember a time when you obeyed God even if you didn't understand why He asked you to do or say something. Tell someone—a son or daughter, a friend or neighbor—about that experience. If you know the result of your obedience, be sure to include that part of the event. Praise the Lord for His direction and let Him know that you trust Him.

Consider It

As you read Luke 4:1–44, consider these questions:

1) What temptations did the devil throw at Jesus?

_____

_____

_____

2) How did Jesus counter these attacks?

_____

_____

_____

3) What did Jesus do after He returned from the wilderness (4:14–15)?

_____

_____

_____

4) What does the prophecy from Isaiah reveal about Jesus' mission (vv. 18–19)?

_____

_____

_____

5) Jesus puts this prophecy into action by healing Peter's mother-in-law and a multitude of others. What does this say about God's character?

_____

_____

_____

6) How does knowing this aspect of God's character affect you?

_____

_____

_____

7) The people try to keep Jesus from leaving (v. 42). What is His response?

_____

_____

_____

Lesson

5

Come Change the World

It's not hard to stay busy. Anyone can do that. But wouldn't you really rather stay busy with a world-changing purpose? Jesus issues an invitation to discover how you can do just that.

Read Luke 5:1–39

Luke 5:1–29

Jesus Calls the First Disciples

5 On one occasion, while the crowd was pressing in on him to hear the word of God, he was standing by the lake of Gennesaret, ²and he saw two boats by the lake, but the fishermen had gone out of them and were washing their nets. ³Getting into one of the boats, which was Simon's, he asked him to put out a little from the land. And he sat down and taught the people from the boat. ⁴And when he had finished speaking, he said to Simon, "Put out into the deep and let down your nets for a catch." ⁵And Simon answered, "Master, we toiled all night and took nothing! But at your word I will let down the nets." ⁶And when they had done this, they enclosed a large number of fish, and their nets were breaking. ⁷They signaled to their partners in the other boat to come and help them. And they came and filled both the boats, so that they began to sink. ⁸But when Simon Peter saw it, he fell down at Jesus' knees, saying, "Depart from me, for I am a sinful man, O Lord." ⁹For he and all who were with him were astonished at the catch of fish that they had taken, ¹⁰and so also were James and John, sons of Zebedee, who were partners with Simon. And Jesus said to Simon, "Do not be afraid; from now on you will be catching men." ¹¹And when they had brought their boats to land, they left everything and followed him.

Jesus Cleanses a Leper

¹²While he was in one of the cities, there came a man full of leprosy. And when he saw Jesus, he fell on his face and begged him, "Lord, if you will, you can make me clean." ¹³And Jesus stretched out his hand and touched him, saying, "I will; be clean." And immediately the leprosy left him. ¹⁴And he charged him to tell no one, but "go

> # Key Verse
>
> *And Jesus said to Simon, "Do not be afraid; from now on you will be catching men"* (Luke 5:10).

and show yourself to the priest, and make an offering for your cleansing, as Moses commanded, for a proof to them." ¹⁵But now even more the report about him went abroad, and great crowds gathered to hear him and to be healed of their infirmities. ¹⁶But he would withdraw to desolate places and pray.

Jesus Heals a Paralytic

¹⁷On one of those days, as he was teaching, Pharisees and teachers of the law were sitting there, who had come from every village of Galilee and Judea and from Jerusalem. And the power of the Lord was with him to heal. ¹⁸And behold, some men were bringing on a bed a man who was paralyzed, and they were seeking to bring him in and lay him before Jesus, ¹⁹but finding no way to bring him in, because of the crowd, they went up on the roof and let him down with his bed through the tiles into the midst before Jesus. ²⁰And when he saw their faith, he said, "Man, your sins are forgiven you." ²¹And the scribes and the Pharisees began to question, saying, "Who is this who speaks blasphemies? Who can forgive sins but God alone?" ²²When Jesus perceived their thoughts, he answered them, "Why do you question in your hearts? ²³Which is easier, to say, 'Your sins are forgiven

you,' or to say, 'Rise and walk'? ²⁴But that you may know that the Son of Man has authority on earth to forgive sins"—he said to the man who was paralyzed—"I say to you, rise, pick up your bed and go home." ²⁵And immediately he rose up before them and picked up what he had been lying on and went home, glorifying God. ²⁶And amazement seized them all, and they glorified God and were filled with awe, saying, "We have seen extraordinary things today."

Jesus Calls Levi

²⁷After this he went out and saw a tax collector named Levi, sitting at the tax booth. And he said to him, "Follow me." ²⁸And leaving everything, he rose and followed him.

²⁹And Levi made him a great feast in his house, and there was a large company of tax collectors and others reclining at table with them.

S teve Jobs, founder of Apple Computers, was trying to recruit John Sculley, who at the time was the 43-year-old president of Pepsi-Cola. Jobs issued a tremendous challenge. He said, "John, do you want to spend the rest of your life selling sugared water or do you want a chance to change the world?" Sculley accepted the challenge and became CEO of Apple in 1983.

Jesus extended a similar challenge to a group of men along the shores of the Sea of Galilee (Gennesaret). It started out as an ordinary day for these men. They had spent all night in a fruitless effort to catch fish. They were disappointed—their livelihood depended on fish. They were exhausted. All they wanted to do was wash their nets, go home, and catch some shuteye. That's when an itinerant preacher named Jesus showed up. Pressed by the crowds, Jesus commandeered one of the fishing boats and had the owner, Peter, put out a little from the land.

After a time of teaching the crowds, He turned to Peter and said, "Put out into the deep and let down your nets for a catch" (Luke 5:4). Peter had heard of Jesus—who hadn't! But here was a carpenter-turned-preacher telling a professional fisherman what to do. Peter's response may have surprised his fellow fishermen: "Master, we

"Are you a busy person? If so, then you're a prime candidate to hear Jesus say, 'Follow me.'"

toiled all night and took nothing! But at your word I will let down the nets." The result was a catch of fish so large Peter had to call for his partners, James and John, to bring the second boat to help him haul it in. Matthew 4:18 tells us that Andrew, Peter's brother, was there as well.

Can you imagine that? These fishermen probably never had such a huge catch. Both boats were so full they could barely make it back to shore. These men probably experienced the greatest success in their fishing careers! So, what did Jesus do? He challenged them to a higher calling. "Follow me, and I will make you fishers of men" (Matt. 4:19). And Luke tells us, "And when they had brought their boats to land, they left everything and followed him" (Luke 5:11).

These men weren't the only ones stopped short in their careers. It was only a bit later that Jesus met a man named Levi (or Matthew). Levi was a tax collector. While tax collecting was a hated occupation (the Jews viewed their tax money as going to support a pagan government), it was also profitable. Every few years the right to collect taxes for a particular region would be auctioned off by Rome to the highest bidder. It was up to the tax collector (also called publicans) to recoup the money they paid plus anything extra they could squeeze out of the people. And with the power of Rome behind them, they could squeeze pretty hard.

Luke tells us that it was while Levi was in the very midst of collecting taxes Jesus intruded into his life (v. 27). Jesus didn't say or do anything fancy; He didn't preach a long sermon on the sin of usury (charging excessive interest) or sing multiple stanzas of an invitational hymn. Jesus simply said "Follow me," and "leaving everything, he [Levi] rose and followed him" (v. 28).

Jesus' first disciples were quite a mixed group. Peter, James, John and Andrew were blue-collar laborers. They fished for a living. Levi was a white-collar professional. He collected taxes. Peter was impetuous and outgoing. Oftentimes he said the wrong thing at the wrong time. John, on the other hand, was quiet and introspective. He thought deeply about the truths he heard from Jesus. Levi, in all probability, was detail oriented and calculating. Profits and losses were his game.

But these men did have at least one thing in common—they "left everything." At the peak of their careers, they left it all to follow Jesus. The fishermen didn't try to take their nets or Levi his tax booth; they put themselves entirely into Jesus' hands and did what He asked.

While we aren't told the details of what every disciple was doing when he was called, it would appear that Jesus never tapped people who weren't busy doing something. As far as we know, no one was was called while withdrawn from the world contemplating the mysteries of the universe. Instead they were busy doing whatever was necessary for them to make a living—and, frequently, being very successful at it.

Are you a busy person? Maybe you're climbing the corporate ladder or raising a family or running your own business. Even if you're retired, you probably have more things to do than time to do them. If so, then you're a prime candidate to hear Jesus say, "Follow me." That doesn't mean He will necessarily call you to leave your job. First He calls you to let Him be your Savior. Then He calls you to reflect His character to the people around you.

But He does call some to leave everything and follow Him—to leave jobs, family, friends, and follow Him to faraway places. If you are in that minority, are you willing to leave it all behind and place yourself into His hands?

In other words, do you want to sell sugar water or change the world?

Go Deeper

Have you ever wondered what happened to the 12 disciples Jesus called to be His inner circle? The only ones the Bible tells us about are Judas and James, the brother of John. Judas hanged himself (Matt. 27:5) and Acts 12:1–2 tells us that Herod Agrippa killed James with the sword. But what about the other ten? The Bible doesn't say, but Church tradition tells us the following:

Peter was crucified at Rome with his head downward.

Matthew (Levi) was slain with a sword in Ethiopia.

Philip was crucified in the city of Hierapolis (in Turkey).

Thomas was run through with a lance at Coromandel in India.

Jude (Thaddaeus or Judas, son of James) was shot to death with arrows.

Simon the Zealot was sawn in half while he ministered in Persia.

James, son of Alphaeus (not to be confused with James, John's brother or James, the brother of Jesus), was thrown from a pinnacle of the temple and then beaten to death with a club.

Bartholomew (Nathanael) was flayed alive.

Andrew was bound to a cross, where he preached to his persecutors until he died.

John was put in a cauldron of boiling oil but escaped death in a miraculous manner and was afterwards exiled to Patmos. He is the only disciple who was not martyred.

These men not only left it all, they gave it all. What are you willing to do? What are you willing to give?

Express It

As a Christian, God has called you to reflect His glory to those around you. What does that mean? It means that we're like mirrors others can look into to see what God is like. So, we need to demonstrate God's characteristics to them. Using a concordance, do a word study in the Bible looking for words like mercy, love, longsuffering, forgiveness, or any other of God's attributes. Ask yourself how you're doing reflecting those qualities.

Consider It

As you read Luke 5:1–39, consider these questions:

1) In Luke 5:1, why were the people crowding to Jesus?

_____

_____

_____

2) How did Peter first respond to Jesus' command to go back to the lake and fish?

_____

_____

_____

3) Why do you think Peter responded to Jesus the way he did after the huge catch?

_____

_____

_____

4) When Jesus healed the leper (Luke 5:13), what did He do that was socially unthinkable?

_____

_____

_____

5) What was Jesus' reason for sending the healed leper to the priest?

_____

_____

_____

6) The disciples we read about in this chapter experienced a similar, drastic life-change when Jesus called them. What was it?

_____

_____

_____

7) What challenges in your life would need to be overcome to respond to a call from Jesus like the disciples experienced?

_____

_____

_____

Who Is the Real God?

Have you ever wondered what God is really like? Is He some cosmic policeman just waiting for you to make a mistake? Is He a kindly old grandfather who looks the other way when you do something wrong? Jesus shows us the true character of God the Father.

Read Luke 6:1–7:50

Luke 6:1–7:23

Jesus Is Lord of the Sabbath

6 On a Sabbath, while he was going through the grainfields, his disciples plucked and ate some heads of grain, rubbing them in their hands. ²But some of the Pharisees said, "Why are you doing what is not lawful to do on the Sabbath?" ³And Jesus answered them, "Have you not read what David did when he was hungry, he and those who were with him: ⁴how he entered the house of God and took and ate the bread of the Presence, which is not lawful for any but the priests to eat, and also gave it to those with him?" ⁵And he said to them, "The Son of Man is lord of the Sabbath."

A Man with a Withered Hand

⁶On another Sabbath, he entered the synagogue and was teaching, and a man was there whose right hand was withered. ⁷And the scribes and the Pharisees watched him, to see whether he would heal on the Sabbath, so that they might find a reason to accuse him. ⁸But he knew their thoughts, and he said to the man with the withered hand, "Come and stand here." And he rose and stood there. ⁹And Jesus said to them, "I ask you, is it lawful on the Sabbath to do good or to do harm, to save life or to destroy it?" ¹⁰And after looking around at them all he said to him, "Stretch out your hand." And he did so, and his hand was restored. ¹¹But they were filled with fury and discussed with one another what they might do to Jesus.

The Twelve Apostles

¹²In these days he went out to the mountain to pray, and all night he continued in prayer to God. ¹³And when day came, he called his disciples and chose from them twelve, whom he named apostles: ¹⁴Simon, whom he named Peter, and Andrew his brother, and James and John, and Philip, and

> # Key Verse
>
> *"Be merciful, even as your Father is merciful"*
> (Luke 6:36).

Bartholomew, ¹⁵and Matthew, and Thomas, and James the son of Alphaeus, and Simon who was called the Zealot, ¹⁶and Judas the son of James, and Judas Iscariot, who became a traitor.

Jesus Ministers to a Great Multitude

¹⁷And he came down with them and stood on a level place, with a great crowd of his disciples and a great multitude of people from all Judea and Jerusalem and the seacoast of Tyre and Sidon, ¹⁸who came to hear him and to be healed of their diseases. And those who were troubled with unclean spirits were cured. ¹⁹And all the crowd sought to touch him, for power came out from him and healed them all.

The Beatitudes

²⁰And he lifted up his eyes on his disciples, and said:

"Blessed are you who are poor, for yours is the kingdom of God.

²¹"Blessed are you who are hungry now, for you shall be satisfied.

"Blessed are you who weep now, for you shall laugh.

²²"Blessed are you when people hate you and when they exclude you and revile you and spurn your name as evil, on account of the Son of Man! ²³Rejoice in that day, and leap for joy, for behold, your reward is great in

heaven; for so their fathers did to the prophets.

Jesus Pronounces Woes

24"But woe to you who are rich, for you have received your consolation.

25"Woe to you who are full now, for you shall be hungry.

"Woe to you who laugh now, for you shall mourn and weep.

26"Woe to you, when all people speak well of you, for so their fathers did to the false prophets.

Love Your Enemies

27"But I say to you who hear, Love your enemies, do good to those who hate you, 28bless those who curse you, pray for those who abuse you. 29To one who strikes you on the cheek, offer the other also, and from one who takes away your cloak do not withhold your tunic either. 30Give to everyone who begs from you, and from one who takes away your goods do not demand them back. 31And as you wish that others would do to you, do so to them.

32"If you love those who love you, what benefit is that to you? For even sinners love those who love them. 33And if you do good to those who do good to you, what benefit is that to you? For even sinners do the same. 34And if you lend to those from whom you expect to receive, what credit is that to you? Even sinners lend to sinners, to get back the same amount. 35But love your enemies, and do good, and lend, expecting nothing in return, and your reward will be great, and you will be sons of the Most High, for he is kind to the ungrateful and the evil. 36Be merciful, even as your Father is merciful.

Judging Others

37"Judge not, and you will not be judged; condemn not, and you will not be condemned; forgive, and you will be forgiven; 38give, and it will be given to you. Good measure, pressed down, shaken together, running over, will be put into your lap. For with the measure you use it will be measured back to you."

39He also told them a parable: "Can a blind man lead a blind man? Will they not both fall into a pit? 40A disciple is not above his teacher, but everyone when he is fully trained will be like his teacher. 41Why do you see the speck that is in your brother's eye, but do not notice the log that is in your own eye? 42How can you say to your brother, 'Brother, let me take out the speck that is in your eye,'when you yourself do not see the log that is in your own eye? You hypocrite, first take the log out of your own eye, and then you will see clearly to take out the speck that is in your brother's eye.

A Tree and Its Fruit

43"For no good tree bears bad fruit, nor again does a bad tree bear good fruit, 44for each tree is known by its own fruit. For figs are not gathered from thornbushes, nor are grapes picked from a bramble bush. 45The good person out of the good treasure of his heart produces good, and the evil person out of his evil treasure produces evil, for out of the abundance of the heart his mouth speaks.

Build Your House on the Rock

46"Why do you call me 'Lord, Lord,'and not do what I tell you? 47Everyone who comes to me and hears my words and does them, I will show you what he is like: 48he is like a man building a house, who dug deep and laid the foundation on the rock. And when a flood arose, the stream broke against that house and could not shake it, because it had been well built. 49But the one who hears and does not do them is like a man who built a house on the ground without a foundation. When the stream broke against it, immediately it fell, and the ruin of that house was great."

Jesus Heals a Centurion's Servant

7 After he had finished all his sayings in the hearing of the people, he entered Capernaum. ²Now a centurion had a servant who was sick and at the point of death, who was highly valued by him. ³When the centurion heard about Jesus, he sent to him elders of the Jews, asking him to come and heal his servant. ⁴And when they came to Jesus, they pleaded with him earnestly, saying, "He is worthy to have you do this for him, ⁵for he loves our nation, and he is the one who built us our synagogue." ⁶And Jesus went with them. When he was not far from the house, the centurion sent friends, saying to him, "Lord, do not trouble yourself, for I am not worthy to have you come under my roof. ⁷Therefore I did not presume to come to you. But say the word, and let my servant be healed. ⁸For I too am a man set under authority, with soldiers under me: and I say to one, 'Go,'and he goes; and to another, 'Come,'and he comes; and to my servant, 'Do this,'and he does it." ⁹When Jesus heard these things, he marveled at him, and turning to the crowd that followed him, said, "I tell you, not even in Israel have I found such faith." ¹⁰And when those who had been sent returned to the house, they found the servant well.

Jesus Raises a Widow's Son

¹¹Soon afterward he went to a town called Nain, and his disciples and a great crowd went with him. ¹²As he drew near to the gate of the town, behold, a man who had died was being carried out, the only son of his mother, and she was a widow, and a considerable crowd from the town was with her. ¹³And when the Lord saw her, he had compassion on her and said to her, "Do not weep." ¹⁴Then he came up and touched the bier, and the bearers stood still. And he said, "Young man, I say to you, arise." ¹⁵And the dead man sat up and began to speak, and Jesus gave him to his mother.

¹⁶Fear seized them all, and they glorified God, saying, "A great prophet has arisen among us!" and "God has visited his people!" ¹⁷And this report about him spread through the whole of Judea and all the surrounding country.

Messengers from John the Baptist

¹⁸The disciples of John reported all these things to him. And John, ¹⁹calling two of his disciples to him, sent them to the Lord, saying, "Are you the one who is to come, or shall we look for another?" ²⁰And when the men had come to him, they said, "John the Baptist has sent us to you, saying, 'Are you the one who is to come, or shall we look for another?'" ²¹In that hour he healed many people of diseases and plagues and evil spirits, and on many who were blind he bestowed sight. ²²And he answered them, "Go and tell John what you have seen and heard: the blind receive their sight, the lame walk, lepers are cleansed, and the deaf hear, the dead are raised up, the poor have good news preached to them. ²³And blessed is the one who is not offended by me."

To *Tell the Truth* was a famous TV game show in the 1950s. It consisted of three contestants who all claimed to be the same person. Four celebrity panelists asked each of them a series of questions and then tried to decide which one was honest about his or her identity. The moment of truth always arrived with the statement: "Will the real (person's name) please stand up."

The Jewish people were facing a similar dilemma. Jesus had been ministering for perhaps as much as a year, and His popularity had spread. The common people flocked to Him bringing those who were physically and spiritually ill. The God that Jesus shared was compassionate. He cared about the hurts and needs of His people.

The Pharisees also had a version of God—a very different version from the one Jesus presented. Their God was very concerned that everyone "crossed their t's" and "dotted their i's" the same way. So, the people had the God represented by Jesus, and they had the God represented by the scribes and the Pharisees. Which was the real God? When the moment of truth came, which God was going to stand up?

As Jesus grew in popularity, He began to develop enemies among the religious elite who preferred the more rigid and demanding view of God. These religious leaders would eventually bring about His death. They were going to make sure their version of God won.

So, what were their complaints? One of the major issues was the Sabbath. To the Jew, the Sabbath (Saturday) was the most important day of the week. In fact, some rabbis taught that the Messiah would not come until Israel perfectly kept the Sabbath. With their strict legalism, the religious leaders had turned the Sabbath into a burden of responsibility instead of a blessing of rest.

When Jesus' disciples picked some grain and ate it on the Sabbath, some of the Pharisees were up in arms. Jesus' response was to turn to God's Word. He pointed out to these fault-finders that God never intended the Law to hinder meeting personal needs. David, the greatest king Israel ever had, broke the Law when he and his men ate the consecrated bread in the Tabernacle (1 Sam. 21:1–6); but they were not condemned.

"When people look at us, what do they see and hear? When we speak words of truth with love, we reveal God's character. When we keep our lives pure, show compassion to those around us, are gracious instead of critical with those with whom we disagree, then we are revealing the glory of God."

On yet another Sabbath, Jesus healed a man with a withered hand. Again, the religious leaders were offended. Not even a miracle could soften their hardened hearts. Compassion was secondary to the Law. From that point on, they "discussed with one another what they might do to Jesus" (Luke 6:11).

Gathering a hand-picked group of disciples (6:12–16), Jesus began a tour of the northern region around the Sea of Galilee to correct people's perception of God. The common people needed to know that the Father was not the legalistic God depicted by the religious leaders.

Jesus continually showed the people the true nature of His Father. The glory of God was not in keeping a legal system but in building a right relationship with Him. Jesus taught them to love their enemies and do good to those who hated them. After all, that's what the Father did. And He taught them not to judge the motives of others. Only God knows the innermost secrets of another person's heart. Jesus taught them to look at their own lives before trying to correct someone else. He urged them to build their lives on the solid rock of His words rather than the shifting sands of other people's opinions.

And so, with many parables and figures of speech, Jesus taught them with authority about the character of the true God.

And He backed up His words with acts of compassion. He healed the centurion's servant (7:1–10) and raised the son of a widow in the city of Nain from the dead (7:11–17). With compassion, He healed those who had diseases, plagues, blindness, and evil spirits. When John the Baptist sent some of his disciples to ask Jesus if He were truly the Messiah, Jesus pointed to His actions and said "Go and tell John what you have seen and heard: the blind receive their sight, the lame walk, lepers are cleansed, and the deaf hear, the dead are raised up, the poor have good news preached to them" (v. 22).

When people look at us, what do they see and hear? When we speak words of truth with love, we reveal God's character. When we keep our lives pure, show compassion to those around us, are gracious instead of critical with those with whom we disagree, then we are revealing the glory of God. If we do that, when it's time for people to identify the real God, the correct answer should be obvious to everyone.

Go Deeper

When God finished the work of creation, He rested (Gen. 2:2). He didn't rest because He was tired; He rested because He was finished (Gen. 2:1–2). Creation was complete. It was in perfect harmony with Him.

But soon that rest was broken. Adam and Eve rebelled against God, and creation was no longer complete. Sin entered the world, and God's creation needed to be brought back into harmony with Him. The Law (the Ten Commandments) was given to Israel as a schoolteacher or guardian (Gal. 3:24).

The fourth commandment set aside a day of rest (the seventh day or Saturday). This was called the Sabbath. The physical rest they experienced on this day was a reminder to the Jewish people of the spiritual rest they lacked.

When we come to the New Testament, we discover the only commandment not repeated was the fourth—"Remember the Sabbath." There's good reason for this. When Jesus finished the work of redemption (John 17:4), He restored the true Sabbath. The rest that existed from Creation to the Fall was available through Him. Jesus said, "Come to me, all you who labor and are heavy laden, and I will give you rest" (Matt. 11:28).

We enter into Christ's rest when we receive Him as our Savior. Keeping the Law never brought salvation, and it never brought rest. Neither does keeping the Sabbath because Jesus became our Sabbath. In Him we have the true Sabbath rest. We acknowledge the completeness of Jesus' salvation for us when we worship on the first day of the week, the day Jesus rose from the dead and all the elements of the Gospel were complete. That resurrection day was the day mankind again could rest in the joy of the Lord. The New Testament Christ-follower doesn't keep the Sabbath rest because we have the Savior's rest.

Express It

Look again at some of the events mentioned in today's passage: the disciples picking grain and eating it; Jesus healing a man with a withered hand, ministering to the multitude, and others. Write one word to describe the quality Jesus showed in each situation, such as understanding or compassion. Do you exhibit some of the same qualities? Ask a family member to recall a time you showed one of the qualities you wrote down.

Consider It

As you read Luke 6:1–7:50, consider these questions:

1) What did the Pharisees criticize Jesus for doing?

_____

_____

_____

2) How did Jesus answer them?

_____

_____

_____

3) According to Jesus, how are we to deal with our enemies?

_____

_____

_____

4) What should be our first step in helping someone with their problems?

_____

_____

_____

5) What does it mean to build your house on the rock?

_____

_____

_____

6) What impressed Jesus about the centurion?

_____

_____

_____

7) Why did Jesus raise the widow's son in Nain?

_____

_____

_____

8) How does Jesus' value system differ from our current world's system? From your values?

_____

_____

_____

Fear Versus Faith

Lots of things in life cause us to fear: serious illness, financial problems, physical danger. But Jesus shows us the appropriate response to those situations—and it's not fear.

Luke 8:1–56

Women Accompanying Jesus

8 Soon afterward he went on through cities and villages, proclaiming and bringing the good news of the kingdom of God. And the twelve were with him, ²and also some women who had been healed of evil spirits and infirmities: Mary, called Magdalene, from whom seven demons had gone out, ³and Joanna, the wife of Chuza, Herod's household manager, and Susanna, and many others, who provided for them out of their means.

The Parable of the Sower

⁴And when a great crowd was gathering and people from town after town came to him, he said in a parable: ⁵"A sower went out to sow his seed. And as he sowed, some fell along the path and was trampled underfoot, and the birds of the air devoured it. ⁶And some fell on the rock, and as it grew up, it withered away, because it had no moisture. ⁷And some fell among thorns, and the thorns grew up with it and choked it. ⁸And some fell into good soil and grew and yielded a hundredfold." As he said these things, he called out, "He who has ears to hear, let him hear."

The Purpose of the Parables

⁹And when his disciples asked him what this parable meant, ¹⁰he said, "To you it has been given to know the secrets of the kingdom of God, but for others they are in parables, so that 'seeing they may not see, and hearing they may not understand.' ¹¹Now the parable is this: The seed is the word of God. ¹²The ones along the path are those who have heard; then the devil comes and takes away the word from their hearts, so that they may not believe and be saved. ¹³And the ones on the rock are those who,

> # Key Verse
>
> But Jesus on hearing this answered him, "Do not fear; only believe, and she will be well" (Luke 8:50).

when they hear the word, receive it with joy. But these have no root; they believe for a while, and in time of testing fall away. ¹⁴And as for what fell among the thorns, they are those who hear, but as they go on their way they are choked by the cares and riches and pleasures of life, and their fruit does not mature. ¹⁵As for that in the good soil, they are those who, hearing the word, hold it fast in an honest and good heart, and bear fruit with patience.

A Lamp Under a Jar

¹⁶"No one after lighting a lamp covers it with a jar or puts it under a bed, but puts it on a stand, so that those who enter may see the light. ¹⁷For nothing is hidden that will not be made manifest, nor is anything secret that will not be known and come to light. ¹⁸Take care then how you hear, for to the one who has, more will be given, and from the one who has not, even what he thinks that he has will be taken away."

Jesus' Mother and Brothers

¹⁹Then his mother and his brothers came to him, but they could not reach him because of the crowd. ²⁰And he was told, "Your mother and your brothers are standing outside, desiring to see you." ²¹But he answered them, "My mother and

my brothers are those who hear the word of God and do it."

Jesus Calms a Storm

²²One day he got into a boat with his disciples, and he said to them, "Let us go across to the other side of the lake." So they set out, ²³and as they sailed he fell asleep. And a windstorm came down on the lake, and they were filling with water and were in danger. ²⁴And they went and woke him, saying, "Master, Master, we are perishing!" And he awoke and rebuked the wind and the raging waves, and they ceased, and there was a calm. ²⁵He said to them, "Where is your faith?" And they were afraid, and they marveled, saying to one another, "Who then is this, that he commands even winds and water, and they obey him?"

Jesus Heals a Man with a Demon

²⁶Then they sailed to the country of the Gerasenes, which is opposite Galilee. ²⁷When Jesus had stepped out on land, there met him a man from the city who had demons. For a long time he had worn no clothes, and he had not lived in a house but among the tombs. ²⁸When he saw Jesus, he cried out and fell down before him and said with a loud voice, "What have you to do with me, Jesus, Son of the Most High God? I beg you, do not torment me." ²⁹For he had commanded the unclean spirit to come out of the man. (For many a time it had seized him. He was kept under guard and bound with chains and shackles, but he would break the bonds and be driven by the demon into the desert.) ³⁰Jesus then asked him, "What is your name?" And he said, "Legion," for many demons had entered him. ³¹And they begged him not to command them to depart into the abyss. ³²Now a large herd of pigs was feeding there on the hillside, and they begged him to let them enter these. So he gave them permission. ³³Then

the demons came out of the man and entered the pigs, and the herd rushed down the steep bank into the lake and were drowned.

³⁴When the herdsmen saw what had happened, they fled and told it in the city and in the country. ³⁵Then people went out to see what had happened, and they came to Jesus and found the man from whom the demons had gone, sitting at the feet of Jesus, clothed and in his right mind, and they were afraid. ³⁶And those who had seen it told them how the demon-possessed man had been healed. ³⁷Then all the people of the surrounding country of the Gerasenes asked him to depart from them, for they were seized with great fear. So he got into the boat and returned. ³⁸The man from whom the demons had gone begged that he might be with him, but Jesus sent him away, saying, ³⁹"Return to your home, and declare how much God has done for you." And he went away, proclaiming throughout the whole city how much Jesus had done for him.

Jesus Heals a Woman and Jairus's Daughter

⁴⁰Now when Jesus returned, the crowd welcomed him, for they were all waiting for him. ⁴¹And there came a man named Jairus, who was a ruler of the synagogue. And falling at Jesus' feet, he implored him to come to his house, ⁴²for he had an only daughter, about twelve years of age, and she was dying.

As Jesus went, the people pressed around him. ⁴³And there was a woman who had had a discharge of blood for twelve years, and though she had spent all her living on physicians,she could not be healed by anyone. ⁴⁴She came up behind him and touched the fringe of his garment, and immediately her discharge of blood ceased. ⁴⁵And Jesus said, "Who was it that touched me?" When all denied it, Peter said, "Master, the crowds surround you and are pressing in on you!" ⁴⁶But Jesus said, "Someone touched me, for I perceive that power has gone out from me." ⁴⁷And when the woman saw that she was not hidden, she came trembling, and falling down before him declared in the presence of all the people why she had touched him, and how she had been immediately healed. ⁴⁸And he said to her, "Daughter, your faith has made you well; go in peace."

⁴⁹While he was still speaking, someone from the ruler's house came and said, "Your daughter is dead; do not trouble the Teacher any more." ⁵⁰But Jesus on hearing this answered him, "Do not fear; only believe, and she will be well." ⁵¹And when he came to the house, he allowed no one to enter with him, except Peter and John and James, and the father and mother of the child. ⁵²And all were weeping and mourning for her, but he said, "Do not weep, for she is not dead but sleeping." ⁵³And they laughed at him, knowing that she was dead. ⁵⁴But taking her by the hand he called, saying, "Child, arise." ⁵⁵And her spirit returned, and she got up at once. And he directed that something should be given her to eat. ⁵⁶And her parents were amazed, but he charged them to tell no one what had happened.

B iologists say that fear is not only a universal emotion, but it's the first emotion to develop in both humans and animals. Make an unexpected loud noise, and an infant will begin to cry in fear. Catch a baby bird, and you will feel its heart beat wildly in terror. The whole of creation is under the dominion of fear. We come into the world with a fear reflex, and that basic fear is multiplied a thousand times as we increase in knowledge and experience.

So, it's hard to find fault with the disciples for their fears. Luke 8 tells us that Jesus and the disciples got into a boat and started across the lake (v. 22). This would have been the Lake of Gennesaret or the Sea of Galilee as it was also called. This body of water is shallow—approximately 150 feet deep at the deepest part. The Galilean hills around it, some of which reach up to 2,000 feet high, can create a wind-tunnel effect. Add the cold air off the high hills and the warm moist air around the lake, and you have a formula for the perfect storm. And it was one of those kinds of storms that hit the disciple's boat. Certainly their natural reaction was fear.

> *"When you trust in the God of glory, the glory of God leaves you with nothing to fear."*

But, fortunately, they knew where to turn. Even though Jesus was sleeping, Luke 8:24 says, "And they went and woke him, saying, 'Master, Master, we are perishing!'" Now, keep in mind that some of these disciples were experienced fishermen. This wasn't the first storm they had been through, so when they thought they were perishing, you know things were serious.

And what was Jesus' response? "And he awoke and rebuked the wind and the raging waves, and they ceased, and there was a calm." But the next verse is the most telling. "He said to them, 'Where is your faith?'" (v. 25).

Consider this: the opposite of fear is not courage; it's faith. The writer of Hebrews describes faith in Hebrews 11:1, "Now faith is the assurance of things hoped for, the conviction of things not seen." Faith is confident trust in God's character no matter what our circumstances. This is what glorifies God.

In addition, we find other events in this chapter that caused people to fear. Jesus cast a legion of demons out of a man and allowed them to enter a herd of pigs. The pigs rushed down a steep bank into the sea and drowned. When the people from the surrounding area heard about it, they "asked him to depart from them, for they were seized with great fear" (Luke 8:37). Can you imagine being afraid of Jesus? What were they afraid of? Perhaps they were afraid Jesus might punish them for having pigs. (Jews weren't supposed to eat pork.) Perhaps there were other sins in their lives they didn't want Jesus to mess with. Whatever the reason, it's evident where there is no faith, there is only fear.

Jesus returned to the other side of the lake and met a man named Jairus, a ruler of the synagogue (i.e., probably the person in charge of arranging the service for the local synagogue). This man's only daughter, a 12-year-old, was seriously ill and dying. In fear and desperation, he sought out Jesus to heal her.

As Jesus moved toward Jairus' home, He met another fearful person—a woman with a flow of blood. She was afraid of being rejected because the blood made her "unclean" (unable to worship at the temple). No teacher or other religious leader would want to touch her because that would make him unclean. So, she tried to touch just the hem of Jesus' garment but found she had no need to fear Jesus. Instead of rejecting her, Jesus healed her.

For Jairus, the delay caused by this woman appeared fatal for his daughter. Someone from his house came up while Jesus was still speaking to the woman and said to Jairus, "Your daughter is dead; do not trouble the Teacher any more" (v. 49).

In both of these situations, Jesus went straight to the heart of the matter. To the woman, he said, "Daughter, your faith has made you well; go in peace" (v. 48). Where there was once fear, there was now peace. Jesus' response to Jairus was, "Do not fear; only believe, and she will be well" (v. 50).

Proceeding to Jairus' home, Jesus was as good as His word. Putting everyone out except the parents, Peter, John, and James, Jesus said to the girl, "Child, arise," and her spirit returned (v. 54).

Jesus demonstrated that He had power over nature, over demons, over sickness, and even over death. That same Jesus is with us today and still retains all His power. When you trust in the God of glory, the glory of God leaves you with nothing to fear.

Go Deeper

Physical sickness came into the world because of Adam's sin. It is a result of the curse. Christ, however, redeemed us from that curse when He died on the cross for our sins. Isaiah 53:5 says:

"But he was wounded for our transgressions; he was crushed for our iniquities; upon him was the chastisement that brought us peace, and with his stripes we are healed."

While some Christians apply this verse both to spiritual healing and physical healing, the context makes it clear that Isaiah is talking about spiritual healing. The curse of Adam's sin has been removed from those who receive Christ as Savior, but the effects of that curse linger until our bodies are redeemed as well as our souls (Rom. 8:23; 1 Cor. 15:23).

Also keep the following in mind:

- The Bible usually records only those times when Jesus chose to heal—not those when He didn't choose to heal. Yet, He must have made that choice. For example, when He healed the invalid in John 5, there were many other sick people present but He healed only one.

- Other times when God chose not to heal are recorded in 2 Corinthians 12:7–8 (Paul) and 1 Timothy 5:23 (Timothy).

- God's intent is not always to free our lives from sickness and trouble but rather to cause us to grow and mature, learning to trust Him in sickness or in health.

Express It

Take your "trust temperature" today. Draw a temperature gauge. Along the side of the gauge, label incremental levels of trust beginning at the bottom with "I have trouble trusting God when I face a difficult time," to "I trust God in all situations." Now, indicate with a red mark where you on the gauge. Are you where you want to be? What can you do to increase your "trust temperature"?

Consider It

As you read Luke 8:1–56, consider these questions:

1) What did the disciples learn about Jesus through the storm?

_____

_____

_____

2) What was the problem with their faith?

_____

_____

_____

3) What do you learn about demons from 8:26–33?

_____

_____

_____

4) What assignment did Jesus give the man who was delivered from the demons?

_____

_____

_____

5) Describe the condition of the woman in the crowd.

_____

_____

_____

6) When Jairus was told his daughter was dead, what did Jesus say to him?

_____

_____

_____

7) How do you respond when you're facing difficult situations in your life? How do you think Jesus would want you to respond?

_____

_____

_____

Lesson

8

Time for a Reality Check

Have you ever needed a reality check? Sometimes our perception doesn't match reality, especially when it comes to following Christ. So, Jesus gives His disciples (and us) a reality check. He shows us and tells us exactly what it means to be His disciple.

Luke 9:1–62

Jesus Sends Out the Twelve Apostles

9 And he called the twelve together and gave them power and authority over all demons and to cure diseases, ²and he sent them out to proclaim the kingdom of God and to heal. ³And he said to them, "Take nothing for your journey, no staff, nor bag, nor bread, nor money; and do not have two tunics. ⁴And whatever house you enter, stay there, and from there depart. ⁵And wherever they do not receive you, when you leave that town shake off the dust from your feet as a testimony against them." ⁶And they departed and went through the villages, preaching the gospel and healing everywhere.

Herod Is Perplexed by Jesus

⁷Now Herod the tetrarch heard about all that was happening, and he was perplexed, because it was said by some that John had been raised from the dead, ⁸by some that Elijah had appeared, and by others that one of the prophets of old had risen. ⁹Herod said, "John I beheaded, but who is this about whom I hear such things?" And he sought to see him.

Jesus Feeds the Five Thousand

¹⁰On their return the apostles told him all that they had done. And he took them and withdrew apart to a town called Bethsaida. ¹¹When the crowds learned it, they followed him, and he welcomed them and spoke to them of the kingdom of God and cured those who had need of healing. ¹²Now the day began to wear away, and the twelve came and said to him, "Send the crowd away to go into the surrounding villages and countryside to find lodging and get provisions, for we are here in a desolate place." ¹³But he said to them, "You give them something

> # Key Verse
>
> *And he said to all, "If anyone would come after me, let him deny himself and take up his cross daily and follow me"*
> (Luke 9:23).

to eat." They said, "We have no more than five loaves and two fish—unless we are to go and buy food for all these people." ¹⁴For there were about five thousand men. And he said to his disciples, "Have them sit down in groups of about fifty each." ¹⁵And they did so, and had them all sit down. ¹⁶And taking the five loaves and the two fish, he looked up to heaven and said a blessing over them. Then he broke the loaves and gave them to the disciples to set before the crowd. ¹⁷And they all ate and were satisfied. And what was left over was picked up, twelve baskets of broken pieces.

Peter Confesses Jesus as the Christ

¹⁸Now it happened that as he was praying alone, the disciples were with him. And he asked them, "Who do the crowds say that I am?" ¹⁹And they answered, "John the Baptist. But others say, Elijah, and others, that one of the prophets of old has risen." ²⁰Then he said to them, "But who do you say that I am?" And Peter answered, "The Christ of God."

Jesus Foretells His Death

²¹And he strictly charged and commanded them to tell this to no one,

²²saying, "The Son of Man must suffer many things and be rejected by the elders and chief priests and scribes, and be killed, and on the third day be raised."

Take Up Your Cross and Follow Jesus

²³And he said to all, "If anyone would come after me, let him deny himself and take up his cross daily and follow me. ²⁴For whoever would save his life will lose it, but whoever loses his life for my sake will save it. ²⁵For what does it profit a man if he gains the whole world and loses or forfeits himself? ²⁶For whoever is ashamed of me and of my words, of him will the Son of Man be ashamed when he comes in his glory and the glory of the Father and of the holy angels. ²⁷But I tell you truly, there are some standing here who will not taste death until they see the kingdom of God."

The Transfiguration

²⁸Now about eight days after these sayings he took with him Peter and John and James and went up on the mountain to pray. ²⁹And as he was praying, the appearance of his face was altered, and his clothing became dazzling white. ³⁰And behold, two men were talking with him, Moses and Elijah, ³¹who appeared in glory and spoke of his departure, which he was about to accomplish at Jerusalem. ³²Now Peter and those who were with him were heavy with sleep, but when they became fully awake they saw his glory and the two men who stood with him. ³³And as the men were parting from him, Peter said to Jesus, "Master, it is good that we are here. Let us make three tents, one for you and one for Moses and one for Elijah"—not knowing what he said. ³⁴As he was saying these things, a cloud came and overshadowed them, and they were afraid as they entered the cloud. ³⁵And a voice came out of the cloud, saying, "This is my Son, my Chosen One; listen to him!" ³⁶And

when the voice had spoken, Jesus was found alone. And they kept silent and told no one in those days anything of what they had seen.

Jesus Heals a Boy with an Unclean Spirit

³⁷On the next day, when they had come down from the mountain, a great crowd met him. ³⁸And behold, a man from the crowd cried out, "Teacher, I beg you to look at my son, for he is my only child. ³⁹And behold, a spirit seizes him, and he suddenly cries out. It convulses him so that he foams at the mouth, and shatters him, and will hardly leave him. ⁴⁰And I begged your disciples to cast it out, but they could not." ⁴¹Jesus answered, "O faithless and twisted generation, how long am I to be with you and bear with you? Bring your son here." ⁴²While he was coming, the demon threw him to the ground and convulsed him. But Jesus rebuked the unclean spirit and healed the boy, and gave him back to his father. ⁴³And all were astonished at the majesty of God.

Jesus Again Foretells His Death

But while they were all marveling at everything he was doing, Jesus said to his disciples, ⁴⁴"Let these words sink into your ears: The Son of Man is about to be delivered into the hands of men." ⁴⁵But they did not understand this saying, and it was concealed from them, so that they might not perceive it. And they were afraid to ask him about this saying.

Who Is the Greatest?

⁴⁶An argument arose among them as to which of them was the greatest. ⁴⁷But Jesus, knowing the reasoning of their hearts, took a child and put him by his side ⁴⁸and said to them, "Whoever receives this child in my name receives me, and whoever receives me receives him who sent me. For he who is least among you all is the one who is great."

Anyone Not Against Us Is For Us

⁴⁹John answered, "Master, we saw someone casting out demons in your name, and we tried to stop him, because he does not follow with us." ⁵⁰But Jesus said to him, "Do not stop him, for the one who is not against you is for you."

A Samaritan Village Rejects Jesus

⁵¹When the days drew near for him to be taken up, he set his face to go to Jerusalem. ⁵²And he sent messengers ahead of him, who went and entered a village of the Samaritans, to make preparations for him. ⁵³But the people did not receive him, because his face was set toward Jerusalem. ⁵⁴And when his disciples James and John saw it, they said, "Lord, do you want us to tell fire to come down from heaven and consume them?" ⁵⁵But he turned and rebuked them. ⁵⁶And they went on to another village.

The Cost of Following Jesus

⁵⁷As they were going along the road, someone said to him, "I will follow you wherever you go." ⁵⁸And Jesus said to him, "Foxes have holes, and birds of the air have nests, but the Son of Man has nowhere to lay his head." ⁵⁹To another he said, "Follow me." But he said, "Lord, let me first go and bury my father." ⁶⁰And Jesus said to him, "Leave the dead to bury their own dead. But as for you, go and proclaim the kingdom of God." ⁶¹Yet another said, "I will follow you, Lord, but let me first say farewell to those at my home." ⁶²Jesus said to him, "No one who puts his hand to the plow and looks back is fit for the kingdom of God."

Oh, the glamour of it all—the miraculous healings, the casting out of demons, being center stage and preaching before crowds of hundreds or even thousands. Think of the excitement, the joy, and yes, even the adoration of the crowds these 12 disciples must have experienced as they set out on their first ministry trip without Jesus. And, being human, they probably loved it. But when they came back to report to Jesus, He showed them the other side of being His disciple.

Being a disciple of Jesus means trusting Him when situations look impossible. The disciples had barely returned from their ministry tour when they went with Jesus to a town called Bethsaida. When the crowds learned of it, they followed, and Jesus welcomed them—all 5,000 of them. But as the day wore on, a problem came up. The crowd apparently had not thought to bring food or perhaps they had eaten it for lunch. It was now getting near evening, and their stomachs were beginning to growl.

"Being a disciple of Jesus means putting Jesus first, deepening your understanding of Him through reading God's Word, growing in your relationship with Him, and making sacrifices for Him."

The disciples' solution was to send them away and let them fend for themselves. Jesus' solution was for the disciples to feed them. How would you have responded? Probably like the disciples: "'We have no more than five loaves and two fish—unless we are to go and buy food for all these people'" (Luke 9:13). Jesus' response was, "Give me what you've got and I'll make it work." And He did. The 5,000 men (not counting women and children) were fed, and there were leftovers to take home. Being a disciple of Jesus meant a change in approach—you minister to people; you don't send them away to fend for themselves.

Being a disciple of Jesus also means a change in priorities—no longer is it "me first," but it's "Jesus first." The Lord says, "If anyone would come after me, let him deny himself and take up his cross daily and follow me" (v. 23). Sometimes we refer to some burden or hardship as a "cross to bear." But crosses were not burdens, they were instruments of death. The apostle Paul says, "It is no longer I who live, but Christ who lives in me. And the life I now live in the flesh I live by faith in the Son of God, who loved me and gave himself for me" (Gal. 2:20). When Paul became a follower of Jesus Christ, his life and will became absorbed in Christ's life and will. He learned to put Christ first. That's true discipleship.

Being a disciple of Jesus also means knowing your Master. A disciple in Jesus' day would often actually move in with his master so he could come to know Him better. He would see his master respond to daily situations. Some of Jesus' disciples had been with Him at this point for at least a couple years. How well did they know Him? Peter put that issue to rest when he declared Jesus was "the Christ of God" (v. 20). How well do you know Jesus?

Being a disciple of Jesus also means sacrifice. Twice in this chapter, Jesus told His disciples that He was going to be killed. Even though they didn't know it at the time, all but one of them would also die for his faith. (See Go Deeper for Luke 5.) Martyrdom is not something a Christian should seek, but if it comes, it's something we need to be prepared to accept.

But even if the ultimate sacrifice is not required, there are other sacrifices a disciple of Jesus must make. One man who wanted to be a disciple said, "'I will follow you wherever you go.'" In effect, Jesus replied, "Oh really? Do you realize I don't even have a place to lay my head?" (vv. 57–58.) Another man whom Jesus called replied, "'Lord, let me first go and bury my father.'" Now, he didn't mean his father had died and he needed to bury him. He meant, "Lord, wait until my father passes away, and then I will follow you." But Jesus said, "'Leave the dead to bury their own dead.'" Yet a third person said, "'I will follow you, Lord, but let me first say farewell to those at my home.'" Of course this could take weeks as various relatives would come from far away and special farewell dinners would be held. (See Gen. 24:54–55.) Learn this lesson well: When Jesus calls you, delay is as good as a denial.

Many people are attracted to Christ by what they think will be the glam and the glory. They like the idea of being the center of attention as they lead a Bible study, head up a program or sing with the worship team. While these all need to be done, they aren't what it means to be a real disciple. Others just want to be known in their community as a moral, church-going person. Nothing wrong with that. But being a disciple of Jesus means more. Being a disciple of Jesus means putting Jesus first, deepening your understanding of Him through reading God's Word, growing in your relationship with Him, and making sacrifices for Him. Are you ready for that? Unless you are, you're really not ready to answer Jesus' call to "Follow me."

Go Deeper

The importance of the Transfiguration can be seen by its inclusion in three of the four Gospels (Matt. 17:1–8; Mark 9:2–8; Luke 9:28–36) and an indirect reference to it in John's Gospel when he writes: "And the Word became flesh and dwelt among us, and we have seen His glory, glory as of the only Son from the Father, full of grace and truth" (John 1:14).

The disciples were convinced that Jesus was "the Christ of God" (Luke 9:20), but the kingdom of God as they pictured it had not appeared. In fact, Jesus followed Peter's confession of His deity by declaring He would be rejected and killed (v. 22). That's not exactly what they had in mind when they thought of the Messiah and His kingdom.

But Jesus also declared that some who were standing there would see His kingdom before they died. This happened eight days later when Jesus took the "inner three"—Peter, John, and James—to a mountaintop. There they saw Christ in dazzling glory and heard Moses and Elijah discussing with Jesus the necessity of His sacrificial death (vv. 29–31).

The Lord's transfiguration gave the three a glimpse of the glory of Christ's kingdom. After Jesus' Resurrection, they understood the reason for Christ's suffering and death. He was the Coming One whom the prophets foretold—the King of Glory and the Savior of the world.

Express It

Go back to the study taking special note of each time a sentence includes the words, "being a disciple." Make a list of the requirements necessary to be a disciple of Christ. Now, write beside each of these categories one step you can take to be a better disciple.

Consider It

As you read Luke 9:1–62, consider these questions:

1) What did Jesus give the disciples as He sent the Twelve out to minister?

_____

_____

_____

2) How did Jesus handle the crowds that followed Him to Bethsaida?

_____

_____

_____

3) How did Peter answer Jesus' big question? Why is this important?

_____

_____

_____

4) What else do the disciples need to understand, based on their knowledge of Jesus?

_____

_____

_____

5) According to Jesus, what makes a person great?

_____

_____

_____

6) Several people came to follow Jesus; what did He say to them?

_____

_____

_____

7) Based on this chapter, is there anything in your life that might need to change in order for you to be a true disciple of Christ? If so, what? What action steps are needed today?

_____

_____

_____

Do Your Duty

Duty may not be a word we like to think about. Duty has a way of leaving a nasty taste in our mouth. Duty is something we do because we have to, not because we want to. But Jesus points us toward a different kind of duty, a duty based on love, not obligation.

Luke 10:1–42

Jesus Sends Out the Seventy-Two

10 After this the Lord appointed seventy-two others and sent them on ahead of him, two by two, into every town and place where he himself was about to go. [2]And he said to them, "The harvest is plentiful, but the laborers are few. Therefore pray earnestly to the Lord of the harvest to send out laborers into his harvest. [3]Go your way; behold, I am sending you out as lambs in the midst of wolves. [4]Carry no moneybag, no knapsack, no sandals, and greet no one on the road. [5]Whatever house you enter, first say, 'Peace be to this house!' [6]And if a son of peace is there, your peace will rest upon him. But if not, it will return to you. [7]And remain in the same house, eating and drinking what they provide, for the laborer deserves his wages. Do not go from house to house. [8]Whenever you enter a town and they receive you, eat what is set before you. [9]Heal the sick in it and say to them, 'The kingdom of God has come near to you.' [10]But whenever you enter a town and they do not receive you, go into its streets and say, [11]"Even the dust of your town that clings to our feet we wipe off against you. Nevertheless know this, that the kingdom of God has come near.' [12]I tell you, it will be more bearable on that day for Sodom than for that town.

Woe to Unrepentant Cities

[13]"Woe to you, Chorazin! Woe to you, Bethsaida! For if the mighty works done in you had been done in Tyre and Sidon, they would have repented long ago, sitting in sackcloth and ashes. [14]But it will be more bearable in the judgment for Tyre and Sidon than for you. [15]And you, Capernaum, will you be exalted to heaven? You shall be brought down to Hades.

[16]"The one who hears you hears me, and the one who rejects you rejects me,

> # Key Verse
>
> "Go your way; behold,
> I am sending you out
> as lambs in the midst of
> wolves" (Luke 10:3).

and the one who rejects me rejects him who sent me."

The Return of the Seventy-Two

[17]The seventy-two returned with joy, saying, "Lord, even the demons are subject to us in your name!" [18]And he said to them, "I saw Satan fall like lightning from heaven. [19]Behold, I have given you authority to tread on serpents and scorpions, and over all the power of the enemy, and nothing shall hurt you. [20]Nevertheless, do not rejoice in this, that the spirits are subject to you, but rejoice that your names are written in heaven."

Jesus Rejoices in the Father's Will

[21]In that same hour he rejoiced in the Holy Spirit and said, "I thank you, Father, Lord of heaven and earth, that you have hidden these things from the wise and understanding and revealed them to little children; yes, Father, for such was your gracious will. [22]All things have been handed over to me by my Father, and no one knows who the Son is except the Father, or who the Father is except the Son and anyone to whom the Son chooses to reveal him."

[23]Then turning to the disciples he said privately, "Blessed are the eyes that see what you see! [24]For I tell you that many prophets and kings desired to see what you see, and did not see it, and to hear what you hear, and did not hear it."

The Parable of the Good Samaritan

²⁵And behold, a lawyer stood up to put him to the test, saying, "Teacher, what shall I do to inherit eternal life?" ²⁶He said to him, "What is written in the Law? How do you read it?" ²⁷And he answered, "You shall love the Lord your God with all your heart and with all your soul and with all your strength and with all your mind, and your neighbor as yourself." ²⁸And he said to him, "You have answered correctly; do this, and you will live."

²⁹But he, desiring to justify himself, said to Jesus, "And who is my neighbor?" ³⁰Jesus replied, "A man was going down from Jerusalem to Jericho, and he fell among robbers, who stripped him and beat him and departed, leaving him half dead. ³¹Now by chance a priest was going down that road, and when he saw him he passed by on the other side. ³²So likewise a Levite, when he came to the place and saw him, passed by on the other side. ³³But a Samaritan, as he journeyed, came to where he was, and when he saw him, he had compassion. ³⁴He went to him and bound up his wounds, pouring on oil and wine. Then he set him on his own animal and brought him to an inn and took care of him. ³⁵And the next day he took out two denarii and gave them to the innkeeper, saying, 'Take care of him, and whatever more you spend, I will repay you when I come back.' ³⁶Which of these three, do you think, proved to be a neighbor to the man who fell among the robbers?" ³⁷He said, "The one who showed him mercy." And Jesus said to him, "You go, and do likewise."

Martha and Mary

³⁸Now as they went on their way, Jesus entered a village. And a woman named Martha welcomed him into her house. ³⁹And she had a sister called Mary, who sat at the Lord's feet and listened to his teaching. ⁴⁰But Martha was distracted with much serving. And she went up to him and said, "Lord, do you not care that my sister has left me to serve alone? Tell her then to help me." ⁴¹But the Lord answered her, "Martha, Martha, you are anxious and troubled about many things, ⁴²but one thing is necessary. Mary has chosen the good portion, which will not be taken away from her."

On October 21, 1805, the British Royal Navy under the command of Admiral Lord Nelson defeated the combined fleets of the French and Spanish navy. The Battle of Trafalgar laid the groundwork for the eventual defeat of Napoleon Bonaparte. Before the battle, Lord Nelson sent this message to all his ships, "England expects that every man will do his duty." Even though Nelson was mortally wounded during the battle, his sailors performed bravely and carried the day. As the Admiral lay dying, his last words were, "Thank God, I have done my duty."

Oftentimes people see a duty as something you do because you have to. But that's not true when love is involved. When you care for someone, doing what he or she needs becomes a delight. That should be the way it is with Jesus. You can imagine Jesus sending us the same message: "I expect you to do your duty." How do you respond? Is it with joy or feelings of obligation?

So, what is a Christian's duty? We get some idea from the stories in this chapter.

There is the duty to proclaim the Gospel. Jesus sent out 72 (some texts read "seventy") of His disciples. These were not the Twelve whom He had sent out earlier, but a group of anonymous followers who were willing to put their lives on the line (sheep among wolves) to declare that the kingdom of God was near. Without money, food, or extra clothing, these disciples were dependent upon the goodwill of the people they met. But Jesus reminds them that if anyone would not receive them, it was the same as not receiving Him. According to Jesus, it will be better for such cities as Sodom, Tyre, and Sidon, all known for their wickedness, than it will be for Chorazin, Bethsaida, and Capernaum who had seen God's glory but rejected it.

As representatives of Christ, we are to proclaim the good news of the Gospel, but we are not responsible for people's acceptance or rejection. At the same time, those who have the opportunity to hear the message of salvation but refuse will stand in greater judgment than those who haven't heard.

There is also the duty to reach out to those in need. Jesus makes this clear with the story of the Good Samaritan (Luke 10:25–37).

"Don't sacrifice the eternal for things that will soon pass away. Do your duty for Jesus today—not because you have to but because you love Him."

The Samaritans were half-breeds. After the ten northern tribes were taken into captivity by the Assyrians in 722 B.C., they were replaced by non-Jews from other countries. The people who were left behind became intermarried with these foreigners. Their bloodline as well as their religion became mixed with paganism. The two southern tribes (Benjamin and Judah) were also taken into exile later by the Babylonians. During their exile, the Jews from these tribes maintained their purity. When they returned, they had no respect for their mixed-breed neighbors. They called them "dogs."

In this story, Jesus delivered a double insult to the religious leaders of His day. First, He cast a priest and a Levite (two men who should have represented God) as the "bad guys." If that wasn't bad enough, He made a hated Samaritan the "good guy." Jesus wanted them to know that religious ideas that weren't being put into practice were worthless. As His half-brother, James, would later say, "Religion that is pure and undefiled before God, the Father, is this: to visit orphans and widows in their affliction, and to keep oneself unstained from the world" (James 1:27).

But a Christian's duty is not all about action. The contrast between Mary and Martha makes this clear (Luke 10:38–42). As Martha scurries about fixing food for Jesus and His disciples, her sister, Mary, is sitting at Jesus' feet listening to Him. Now, to be honest, don't you feel put out when you're working hard and someone else seems to be taking it easy? Well, Martha did, and she went right to the top to express her unhappiness. You can imagine Martha standing squarely in front of Jesus, both hands on her hips, saying, "Lord, do you not care that my sister has left me to serve alone?" (v. 40).

I'm sure Jesus must have been smiling on the inside as He saw this little Jewish woman taking on the God of the Universe, but He also needed to set her straight. "'Martha, Martha,' He said, 'You are anxious and troubled about many things, but one thing is necessary. Mary has chosen the good portion, which will not be taken away from her.'"

Jesus didn't rebuke Martha for fixing food and doing what she could to make Him and His disciples comfortable. That's important. But it's only temporary. The food will be eaten, and the guests will leave. These things are not worthy of becoming anxious and troubled about. What's really important is the Word of God. Jesus said, "Heaven and earth will pass away, but my words will not pass away" (Matt. 24:35). Don't sacrifice the eternal for things that will soon pass away.

All of us will have to stand before our Lord someday. When we do, we want to be able to say as did Lord Nelson, "Thank God, I have done my duty." Do your duty for Jesus today—not because you have to but because you love Him.

Go Deeper

Signs and wonders (acts that can't be explained by natural means) were common at certain times in the Bible. In the Old Testament, we find them during the Exodus and in the days of Elijah and Elisha. In the New Testament, they occurred during the time of Christ's ministry and the beginning of the Church (the Book of Acts). When these amazing events took place, it was always with the purpose of proving that the message and the messenger were from God. God never gave signs and wonders to feed people's egos, for their personal gain, or simply to amaze the crowds.

But signs and wonders have their limitations. When Jesus fed the crowds, people began to follow Him for the wrong reasons (John 6:26). People gathered to be entertained rather than hear the Gospel.

In the story of Lazarus and the rich man (Luke 16:19–31), the rich man died and went to hell while Lazarus went to paradise (the bosom of Abraham). From the midst of the fire, the rich man asked Abraham to send Lazarus back to warn his brothers. Abraham said, "If they do not hear Moses and the Prophets, neither will they be convinced if someone should rise from the dead" (v. 31). Miracles don't bring repentance.

Instead of signs and wonders, God has given us the Bible. This is what convicts people of their sins. The writer of Hebrews says, "For the word of God is living and active, sharper than any two-edged sword, piercing to the division of soul and of spirit, of joints and of marrow, and discerning the thoughts and intentions of the heart" (Heb. 4:12). The Word is far more effective than signs and wonders.

Express It

In the story of Martha and Mary, we learn the best part of serving Christ is the closeness of that special relationship between Him and us. How long has it been since you took a few hours just to savor being with Christ? It's nearly impossible to create any spare time in the course of our busy lives, but schedule an hour or more to get away and be alone with the Lord. Take your lawn chair and your Bible and find a spot in a park, beside a lake or somewhere else that's quiet where you can read and pray and enjoy God's creation.

Consider It

As you read Luke 10:1–42, consider these questions:

1) Jesus said that it will be more bearable for such pagan cities as Tyre, Sidon, and even Sodom than for such Jewish cities as Chorazin, Bethsaida, and Capernaum. Why? How does this apply to you?

_____

_____

2) When the 72 returned, they were rejoicing over the success of their ministry. What did Jesus tell them to rejoice over?

_____

_____

3) What did Jesus rejoice over in His prayer to the Father?

_____

_____

4) Why did Jesus tell the parable of the Good Samaritan?

_____

_____

5) What lessons do you take away from the story of the Good Samaritan?

_____

_____

6) How would you describe Martha?

_____

_____

7) Martha and Mary each made choices about Jesus. Which one best reflects you?

_____

_____

8) What do you do when the duties of "life" conflict with your duties to Jesus?

_____

_____

Lesson
10

Religion or Relationship

Religion is man's effort to reach God. It's built on rules and regulations all geared to please God. God offers us something much better. He offers us a relationship.

Read Luke 11:1–12:58

Luke 11:1–54

The Lord's Prayer

11 Now Jesus was praying in a certain place, and when he finished, one of his disciples said to him, "Lord, teach us to pray, as John taught his disciples." ²And he said to them, "When you pray, say:

"Father, hallowed be your name.
Your kingdom come.

³ Give us each day our daily bread,

⁴ and forgive us our sins,
for we ourselves forgive everyone who is indebted to us.
And lead us not into temptation."

⁵And he said to them, "Which of you who has a friend will go to him at midnight and say to him, 'Friend, lend me three loaves, ⁶for a friend of mine has arrived on a journey, and I have nothing to set before him'; ⁷and he will answer from within, 'Do not bother me; the door is now shut, and my children are with me in bed. I cannot get up and give you anything'? ⁸I tell you, though he will not get up and give him anything because he is his friend, yet because of his impudence he will rise and give him whatever he needs. ⁹And I tell you, ask, and it will be given to you; seek, and you will find; knock, and it will be opened to you. ¹⁰For everyone who asks receives, and the one who seeks finds, and to the one who knocks it will be opened. ¹¹What father among you, if his son asks for a fish, will instead of a fish give him a serpent; ¹²or if he asks for an egg, will give him a scorpion? ¹³If you then, who are evil, know how to give good gifts to your children, how much more will the heavenly Father give the Holy Spirit to those who ask him!"

Jesus and Beelzebul

¹⁴Now he was casting out a demon that was mute. When the demon had gone out, the mute man spoke, and the people marveled. ¹⁵But some of

> # Key Verse
>
> *"But woe to you Pharisees! For you tithe mint and rue and every herb, and neglect justice and the love of God. These you ought to have done, without neglecting the others"* (Luke 11:42).

them said, "He casts out demons by Beelzebul, the prince of demons," ¹⁶while others, to test him, kept seeking from him a sign from heaven. ¹⁷But he, knowing their thoughts, said to them, "Every kingdom divided against itself is laid waste, and a divided household falls. ¹⁸And if Satan also is divided against himself, how will his kingdom stand? For you say that I cast out demons by Beelzebul. ¹⁹And if I cast out demons by Beelzebul, by whom do your sons cast them out? Therefore they will be your judges. ²⁰But if it is by the finger of God that I cast out demons, then the kingdom of God has come upon you. ²¹When a strong man, fully armed, guards his own palace, his goods are safe; ²²but when one stronger than he attacks him and overcomes him, he takes away his armor in which he trusted and divides his spoil. ²³Whoever is not with me is against me, and whoever does not gather with me scatters.

Return of an Unclean Spirit

²⁴"When the unclean spirit has gone out of a person, it passes through waterless places seeking rest, and finding none it says, 'I will return to my house from which I came.' ²⁵And when it comes, it finds the house swept and

put in order. ²⁶Then it goes and brings seven other spirits more evil than itself, and they enter and dwell there. And the last state of that person is worse than the first."

True Blessedness

²⁷As he said these things, a woman in the crowd raised her voice and said to him, "Blessed is the womb that bore you, and the breasts at which you nursed!" ²⁸But he said, "Blessed rather are those who hear the word of God and keep it!"

The Sign of Jonah

²⁹When the crowds were increasing, he began to say, "This generation is an evil generation. It seeks for a sign, but no sign will be given to it except the sign of Jonah. ³⁰For as Jonah became a sign to the people of Nineveh, so will the Son of Man be to this generation. ³¹The queen of the South will rise up at the judgment with the men of this generation and condemn them, for she came from the ends of the earth to hear the wisdom of Solomon, and behold, something greater than Solomon is here. ³²The men of Nineveh will rise up at the judgment with this generation and condemn it, for they repented at the preaching of Jonah, and behold, something greater than Jonah is here.

The Light in You

³³"No one after lighting a lamp puts it in a cellar or under a basket, but on a stand, so that those who enter may see the light. ³⁴Your eye is the lamp of your body. When your eye is healthy, your whole body is full of light, but when it is bad, your body is full of darkness. ³⁵Therefore be careful lest the light in you be darkness. ³⁶If then your whole body is full of light, having no part dark, it will be wholly bright, as when a lamp with its rays gives you light."

Woes to the Pharisees and Lawyers

³⁷While Jesus was speaking, a Pharisee asked him to dine with him, so he went in and reclined at table. ³⁸The Pharisee was astonished to see that he did not first wash before dinner. ³⁹And the Lord said to him, "Now you Pharisees cleanse the outside of the cup and of the dish, but inside you are full of greed and wickedness. ⁴⁰You fools! Did not he who made the outside make the inside also? ⁴¹But give as alms those things that are within, and behold, everything is clean for you.

⁴²"But woe to you Pharisees! For you tithe mint and rue and every herb, and neglect justice and the love of God. These you ought to have done, without neglecting the others. ⁴³Woe to you Pharisees! For you love the best seat in the synagogues and greetings in the marketplaces. ⁴⁴Woe to you! For you are like unmarked graves, and people walk over them without knowing it."

⁴⁵One of the lawyers answered him, "Teacher, in saying these things you insult us also." ⁴⁶And he said, "Woe to you lawyers also! For you load people with burdens hard to bear, and you yourselves do not touch the burdens with one of your fingers. ⁴⁷Woe to you! For you build the tombs of the prophets whom your fathers killed. ⁴⁸So you are witnesses and you consent to the deeds of your fathers, for they killed them, and you build their tombs. ⁴⁹Therefore also the Wisdom of God said, 'I will send them prophets and apostles, some of whom they will kill and persecute,' ⁵⁰so that the blood of all the prophets, shed from the foundation of the world, may be charged against this generation, ⁵¹from the blood of Abel to the blood of Zechariah, who perished between the altar and the sanctuary. Yes, I tell you, it will be required of this generation. ⁵²Woe to you lawyers! For you have taken away the key of knowledge. You did not enter yourselves, and you hindered those who were entering."

⁵³As he went away from there, the scribes and the Pharisees began to press him hard and to provoke him to speak about many things, ⁵⁴lying in wait for him, to catch him in something he might say.

God is all about relationships. God is a Trinity—that means He exists as three persons in one Godhead. For all of eternity, the Father, Son, and Holy Spirit have related to one another in love and with mutual respect. When God created humans, He said, "Let us make man in our image" (Gen. 1:26). Since we are made in the image of God, we, too, have the ability to have relationships. And most importantly, God wants a relationship with you and me.

Religion tries to relate to God through a list of do's and don'ts. The Jewish rabbis took God's Ten Commandments and turned them into 613 commandments. While their sincerity is not in question, their actions didn't result in a relationship. You may obey the law to keep out of trouble with the police, but to say that you and the police have a relationship is not exactly accurate.

God, on the other hand, through His Son, Jesus, and the Holy Spirit, has reached down to offer those who are willing a relationship similar to what is shared within the Godhead. Jesus' death on the cross cleared away the sin that was blocking a relationship between God and us. The Holy Spirit now living in us provides the power for us to live daily in that relationship. But what is our part? Good question. Jesus has the answer.

If we are going to experience all that a relationship with God offers, we can't neglect prayer. While on earth, Jesus made it a point to keep in regular contact with His Father through prayer. In fact, prayer was such a major part of His life, the disciples came to Him and said, "Lord, teach us to pray, as John taught his disciples" (Luke 11:1).

In response, Jesus taught them what we often call the Lord's Prayer, although it might be more accurate to call it the Disciple's Prayer. He taught them to begin praying by relating to God as their "Father." That's the name a child would call his earthly father. It implies a relationship that depends on God the way a child depends on his or her earthly father.

Then Jesus encouraged the disciples to express reverence ("hallowed be your name"). The word *hallow* means "to show respect or treat as holy." In the Bible, a name was the same as the person; to

> *"The one fact we can be sure of is that Christ will return. That means our relationship with God needs to be at the top of our priority list every day."*

hallow God's name means to treat Him with respect. The Father is not your buddy; He is the sovereign God of the universe. We are to treat Him as such.

Jesus also points out that our relationship with the Father entitles us to look forward to His kingdom ("Your kingdom come"), to have our needs met ("Give us each day our daily bread"), to be forgiven ("forgive us our sins") and to receive guidance ("lead us not into temptation").

But our relationship not only involves communicating with God through prayer, it also involves obedience. Jesus says, "Blessed rather are those who hear the word of God and keep it!" (v. 28). Just like in an earthly family, disobedience always puts a strain on our relationships. While it won't get us kicked out of the family (we won't lose our salvation), disobedience will destroy the sense of closeness and joy we would otherwise experience.

Obedience is good; in fact, it's necessary. But how do we know what to obey? That's why we read the Bible. God's Word is our guide for right living, for living a life that pleases God and benefits others. If we don't read our Bibles, we are left in a maze of voices telling us what's right or what's wrong. We need to know for sure and that's why, when it comes to the Bible, we need to read it and to heed it.

Our relationship with God also involves a practical consistency between our words and our actions—as some would say, "Walking the talk." Inconsistency marked the lives of the Pharisees and lawyers (scribes). Jesus accused them of being careful to tithe even such small items as the herbs from their gardens but neglecting the more important issues of justice and love. They claimed to love God, but they killed the apostles (messengers) and prophets God sent (11:47–51). Their walk didn't match their talk.

Just as important, our relationship with God involves a sense of expectancy, even longing, for His return. Jesus said, "You also must be ready, for the Son of Man is coming at an hour you do not expect" (12:40). This sense of expectancy makes our relationship with God exciting and keeps it from becoming stale. If we really believed the Lord Jesus could return today, we'd live like it.

At the same time, these verses should warn us about date-setting. From cults to radio preachers, many have had a crack at setting a date for Christ's return. In the past century, there were at least 93 predictions of Christ's return—some giving specific dates, others indicating a general time period covering several years. So far the only thing these date-setters have in common is the embarrassment of having predicted when Jesus would return only to discover He was not following their timetable.

The one fact we can be sure of, however, is that Christ *will* return (Acts 1:11). That means our relationship with God needs to be at the top of our priority list every day. First John 2:28 urges us: "And now, little children, abide in him, so that when he appears we may have confidence and not shrink from him in shame at his coming." Whether we are caught up in the Rapture, when Jesus removes His Church from the Earth, or pass into the arms of Jesus through the experience of death, we must do all we can to make our relationship with God as intimate as possible.

Go Deeper

Some people like to set up a conflict between Paul and James. They claim that Paul teaches salvation by grace (Eph. 2:8–9) while James requires works (James 2:17). The deeper implication is that the Bible contradicts itself. A closer examination shows this is not true.

James never says salvation comes through works. James 2:17 says, "So also faith by itself, if it does not have works, is dead." In other words, a saving faith produces works the way a fruit tree produces fruit. The fruit doesn't give life to the tree; it simply shows that the tree is alive and healthy. James doesn't say we're saved by works, but he says we show our salvation through the works we do (see James 2:18).

But does the apostle Paul have any place for works? The answer is a definite yes. The often quoted Ephesians 2:8–9 establishes we are saved by grace apart from works. This is an essential truth. But Ephesians 2:8–9 should never be quoted apart from verse 10. Ephesians 2:10 says: "For we are his workmanship, created in Christ Jesus for good works, which God prepared beforehand, that we should walk in them."

Paul declares that God wants us to participate in good works not in order to be saved but because we are saved. Just as Jesus reflected the glory of God through the good works He did, so should you and I. When people look at us, they should see God's love and compassion. How? By the good works we do.

There is no conflict between Paul and James, or between works and grace. As with other supposed contradictions, the solution lies in understanding what the Bible truly says.

Express It

Christ promised He would return. What preparations have you made for that certain event? Why not prepare a goal sheet for yourself? Write down at least ten preparations you'd like to make before you see Christ face-to-face. Consider first your relationship with Him. Do you need to ask forgiveness for something? Is there an area of disobedience in your life?

Now, consider your relationship with others. Do you need to share your faith with a neighbor or friend? Do you need to go to someone and ask forgiveness for something? Should you be praying more consistently for a family member? When you've reached a goal, mark it off your list, thank God for helping you achieve it and go on to another one.

Consider It

As you read Luke 11:1–12:58, consider these questions:

1) When we consider the Lord's Prayer, which parts relate to God? Which parts relate to us? Which parts relate to others?

_____

_____

_____

2) After the Lord's Prayer, Jesus tells a parable. What does this parable tell us about prayer?

_____

_____

_____

3) How does Jesus shock the Pharisee at dinner? What is Jesus' response?

_____

_____

_____

4) What does Jesus teach us about His coming?

_____

_____

_____

5) What can we do to be ready? What does that mean in your life?

_____

_____

_____

6) What does Jesus want to find when He returns (12:41–44)?

_____

_____

_____

7) What are the consequences (12:47–48) of not acting according to God's will? How does this apply to you?

_____

_____

_____

Legalism

We've all met them. Maybe they are coworkers; maybe they're in your church. But one thing they have in common is they are sure they have the inside track with God. Follow their rules, and you'll be on God's "most favored" list. Jesus, however, had a different perspective.

Read Luke 13:1–14:34

Luke 13:1–14:6

Repent or Perish

13 There were some present at that very time who told him about the Galileans whose blood Pilate had mingled with their sacrifices. ²And he answered them, "Do you think that these Galileans were worse sinners than all the other Galileans, because they suffered in this way? ³No, I tell you; but unless you repent, you will all likewise perish. ⁴Or those eighteen on whom the tower in Siloam fell and killed them: do you think that they were worse offenders than all the others who lived in Jerusalem? ⁵No, I tell you; but unless you repent, you will all likewise perish."

The Parable of the Barren Fig Tree

⁶And he told this parable: "A man had a fig tree planted in his vineyard, and he came seeking fruit on it and found none. ⁷And he said to the vinedresser, 'Look, for three years now I have come seeking fruit on this fig tree, and I find none. Cut it down. Why should it use up the ground?' ⁸And he answered him, 'Sir, let it alone this year also, until I dig around it and put on manure. ⁹Then if it should bear fruit next year, well and good; but if not, you can cut it down.'"

A Woman with a Disabling Spirit

¹⁰Now he was teaching in one of the synagogues on the Sabbath. ¹¹And there was a woman who had had a disabling spirit for eighteen years. She was bent over and could not fully straighten herself. ¹²When Jesus saw her, he called her over and said to her, "Woman, you are freed from your disability." ¹³And he laid his hands on her, and immediately she was made straight, and she glorified God. ¹⁴But the ruler of the synagogue, indignant because Jesus had healed on the Sabbath, said to the people, "There are six days in which work ought to be done. Come on those days and be

Key Verse

And he said to them, "Which of you, having a son or an ox that has fallen into a well on a Sabbath day, will not immediately pull him out?" (Luke 14:5).

healed, and not on the Sabbath day." ¹⁵Then the Lord answered him, "You hypocrites! Does not each of you on the Sabbath untie his ox or his donkey from the manger and lead it away to water it? ¹⁶And ought not this woman, a daughter of Abraham whom Satan bound for eighteen years, be loosed from this bond on the Sabbath day?" ¹⁷As he said these things, all his adversaries were put to shame, and all the people rejoiced at all the glorious things that were done by him.

The Mustard Seed and the Leaven

¹⁸He said therefore, "What is the kingdom of God like? And to what shall I compare it? ¹⁹It is like a grain of mustard seed that a man took and sowed in his garden, and it grew and became a tree, and the birds of the air made nests in its branches."

²⁰And again he said, "To what shall I compare the kingdom of God? ²¹It is like leaven that a woman took and hid in three measures of flour, until it was all leavened."

The Narrow Door

²²He went on his way through towns and villages, teaching and journeying

toward Jerusalem. ²³And someone said to him, "Lord, will those who are saved be few?" And he said to them, ²⁴"Strive to enter through the narrow door. For many, I tell you, will seek to enter and will not be able. ²⁵When once the master of the house has risen and shut the door, and you begin to stand outside and to knock at the door, saying, 'Lord, open to us,'then he will answer you, 'I do not know where you come from.' ²⁶Then you will begin to say, 'We ate and drank in your presence, and you taught in our streets.' ²⁷But he will say, 'I tell you, I do not know where you come from. Depart from me, all you workers of evil!' ²⁸In that place there will be weeping and gnashing of teeth, when you see Abraham and Isaac and Jacob and all the prophets in the kingdom of God but you yourselves cast out. ²⁹And people will come from east and west, and from north and south, and recline at table in the kingdom of God. ³⁰And behold, some are last who will be first, and some are first who will be last."

Lament over Jerusalem

³¹At that very hour some Pharisees came and said to him, "Get away from here, for Herod wants to kill you." ³²And he said to them, "Go and tell that fox,

'Behold, I cast out demons and perform cures today and tomorrow, and the third day I finish my course. ³³Nevertheless, I must go on my way today and tomorrow and the day following, for it cannot be that a prophet should perish away from Jerusalem.' ³⁴O Jerusalem, Jerusalem, the city that kills the prophets and stones those who are sent to it! How often would I have gathered your children together as a hen gathers her brood under her wings, and you would not! ³⁵Behold, your house is forsaken. And I tell you, you will not see me until you say, 'Blessed is he who comes in the name of the Lord!'"

Healing of a Man on the Sabbath

14 One Sabbath, when he went to dine at the house of a ruler of the Pharisees, they were watching him carefully. ²And behold, there was a man before him who had dropsy. ³And Jesus responded to the lawyers and Pharisees, saying, "Is it lawful to heal on the Sabbath, or not?" ⁴But they remained silent. Then he took him and healed him and sent him away. ⁵And he said to them, "Which of you, having a son or an ox that has fallen into a well on a Sabbath day, will not immediately pull him out?" ⁶And they could not reply to these things.

Jesus began this series of teachings with the story of an unfruitful fig tree. In His day, the fig tree was a well-known symbol of Israel. So, it was pretty clear to His audience who He was talking about.

Jesus indicated this fig tree had been well cared for. It was not a wild fig tree; it had been purposefully planted in a choice spot—a vineyard. That meant it got the same tender care and attention the vines did. But it still didn't produce fruit. After waiting three years, the owner of the vineyard decided to cut it down. If the fig tree wasn't going to produce figs, why should it take up space?

It was only the intervention of the vinedresser (the one who took care of the grapevines) that saved it. He struck a deal with the owner. If the owner would give the tree one more year, the vinedresser agreed to dig around it and apply fertilizer. If the tree still didn't produce fruit, the owner could cut it down.

Jesus told the parable to make the point that God (the owner) would not tolerate unfruitfulness forever. It was directed at the Jewish people and especially the religious leaders of Israel. They were privileged to be the Chosen People of God and receive messages from Him through their prophets. But instead of producing the fruit of God's character (love, compassion, holiness, etc.), they remained barren. They didn't show God's glory to the nations around them.

What caused steadfast Jews and their religious leaders to be so unproductive? If you look at Jesus' encounters with the religious leaders of His day, you'll find that a major cause for Israel's barrenness was what today we would call legalism. These two chapters show Jesus running into this head-on, especially over the issue of the Sabbath.

In Luke 13:10–17, Jesus was teaching in the synagogue on a Sabbath. While there, He noticed a woman with a disabling spirit who was unable to straighten up. She had been like that for the last 18 years. Out of compassion, Jesus called her over and said "Woman, you are freed from your disability" (13:12). Immediately, she was healed and glorified God. The ruler of the synagogue, however, was angry. Rather than seeing this act of compassion as a reflection of God's character (His glory), he scolded the people for seeking healing on the Sabbath.

Luke 14:1–6 tells us on another occasion Jesus went to eat at the home of a ruler of the Pharisees. Again it was on the Sabbath. In addition to other Pharisees and some scribes, there was a man with dropsy (an abnormal collection of fluid causing the body to swell). Jesus healed the man and before the accusations could begin to fly, He said, "Which of you, having a son or an ox that has fallen into a well on a Sabbath day, will not immediately pull him out?" (14:5). The religious leaders knew they all would, so they kept silent.

"God is working in every believer to make us the person He wants us to be."

Legalism tries to relate to God through rules rather than through the Spirit. While it has the appearance of deep spirituality, it actually is deadening not only on the person practicing it but on those around him or her. It claims to honor God, but it really replaces the work of the Holy Spirit with the works of men.

It's easier to see legalism in others than ourselves, but could it be true of you? Let's look at some of the signs of legalism.

Legalism tries to control externals (it's easier to *do* something than *be* something) and majors on the minors. Jesus says to the Pharisees, "But woe to you Pharisees! For you tithe mint and rue and every herb, and neglect justice and the love of God" (Luke 11:42). Legalism starts on the outside with actions and tries to work inward; on the other hand, Jesus wants us to start on the inside and let our faith produce outward actions.

Furthermore, legalism places "rules" ahead of the needs of others or our own needs for that matter. The woman who couldn't straighten her back (13:10–17) and the man with dropsy (14:1–6) were in serious need. But to the legalistic Pharisees, meeting their needs was not as important as keeping the Sabbath.

Perhaps the most damaging characteristic of legalism is it presents a false picture of God. God is presented as a harsh taskmaster who is mainly concerned with what you do. Ominously, He stands nearby, ready to slap you down if you misstep. And if you don't perform, you'll never make it to heaven.

Such a distorted picture of God has kept many people from enjoying a relationship with Jesus. Knowing they could never live up to all the rules the legalists say are necessary to please God, they simply don't try.

The good news is this picture is false. God accepts you where you are and with mercy and grace moves you to where you need to be. His

Spirit will work in you to change the inside which eventually will affect the outside.

When you look at others, keep this in mind: We are all works in progress. Some may be nearer to completion than others, but God is working in every believer to make us the person He wants us to be. Show your brothers and sisters the same mercy and grace that God is showing you. That's the glory of God.

If you haven't already, trust Jesus as your Savior today and discover that it's not about a set of rules but a satisfying relationship. The Bible isn't a rulebook that you memorize; it's an open door to a never-ending relationship that will meet your deepest needs.

Go Deeper

Jesus and His disciples spent much of their time in the open air where crowds of people could gather. No matter what their religious leanings, Jews and Gentiles, rich and poor, healthy and ill could mingle outdoors. Christ's teaching was available to all.

Yet there were also well-established places where faithful Jews could gather for prayer, reading of Scripture, and teaching. These were called synagogues. Jesus often attended and taught there. Luke 4:14–16 says: "And Jesus returned in the power of the Spirit to Galilee, and a report about him went out through all the surrounding country. And he taught in their synagogues, being glorified by all. And he came to Nazareth, where he had been brought up. And as was his custom, he went to the synagogue on the Sabbath day, and he stood up to read."

It was in the synagogues that Jesus met some of His bitterest opponents. They were the ones who knew the Law and the Prophets (the Old Testament) the best. A few respected Him and understood His teachings (Luke 8:41–42); most simply saw Him as a rebel and a lawbreaker (6:6–11).

The synagogues played an important part during the beginning of the early Church (Acts 9:20; 13:5; 13:43; 14:1; etc.). The apostle Paul and his coworkers made the synagogue their first stop in most cities on their missionary journeys. As a trained rabbi, Paul had the right to stand up in the synagogue, read out of the Torah, and then teach the truth of God. Without the synagogues, it would have been very difficult for local churches to take root. When some Jews objected to Paul's interpretation of the Law, they forced him out of the synagogues, but many who believed went with him and fledgling churches were formed.

Express It

Write out your own definition for legalism. List some of the attitudes you see in those who confronted Jesus in this study. What kind of fruit does legalism produce? Is there an area where you struggle with this problem? Take some time to ask God to show you how to make a change in your attitude so you are pleasing to Him and don't fall into legalism in any area of your life.

Consider It

As you read Luke 13:1–14:34, consider these questions:

1) What is the core problem in the parable of the fig tree?

2) What does this tell you about God's approach to us?

3) In the healing of the woman with a disabling spirit, notice when and where Jesus is teaching. What is important about this?

4) What is most important to the ruler of the synagogue? How does this compare to what's important to Jesus?

5) How did the common people respond to the woman's healing?

6) Compare the healing of the woman with a disabling spirit to the man with dropsy. What are the differences? What are the similarities?

7) In what areas might a Christian become legalistic today? Do you struggle with any of these?

Lost and Found

Nowhere is God's glory revealed more certainly than in His attitude toward those who are lost. God doesn't hesitate to search the reject pile if it means finding and saving one lost sinner.

Luke 15:1–32

The Parable of the Lost Sheep

15 Now the tax collectors and sinners were all drawing near to hear him. ²And the Pharisees and the scribes grumbled, saying, "This man receives sinners and eats with them."

³So he told them this parable: ⁴"What man of you, having a hundred sheep, if he has lost one of them, does not leave the ninety-nine in the open country, and go after the one that is lost, until he finds it? ⁵And when he has found it, he lays it on his shoulders, rejoicing. ⁶And when he comes home, he calls together his friends and his neighbors, saying to them, 'Rejoice with me, for I have found my sheep that was lost.' ⁷Just so, I tell you, there will be more joy in heaven over one sinner who repents than over ninety-nine righteous persons who need no repentance.

The Parable of the Lost Coin

⁸"Or what woman, having ten silver coins, if she loses one coin, does not light a lamp and sweep the house and seek diligently until she finds it? ⁹And when she has found it, she calls together her friends and neighbors, saying, 'Rejoice with me, for I have found the coin that I had lost.' ¹⁰Just so, I tell you, there is joy before the angels of God over one sinner who repents."

The Parable of the Prodigal Son

¹¹And he said, "There was a man who had two sons. ¹²And the younger of them said to his father, 'Father, give me the share of property that is coming to me.' And he divided his property between them. ¹³Not many days later, the younger son gathered all he had and took a journey into a far country, and there he squandered his property in reckless living. ¹⁴And when he had spent everything, a severe famine arose in that

> ## Key Verse
>
> *"Just so, I tell you, there will be more joy in heaven over one sinner who repents than over ninety-nine righteous persons who need no repentance"* (Luke 15:7).

country, and he began to be in need. ¹⁵So he went and hired himself out to one of the citizens of that country, who sent him into his fields to feed pigs. ¹⁶And he was longing to be fed with the pods that the pigs ate, and no one gave him anything.

¹⁷"But when he came to himself, he said, 'How many of my father's hired servants have more than enough bread, but I perish here with hunger! ¹⁸I will arise and go to my father, and I will say to him, "Father, I have sinned against heaven and before you. ¹⁹I am no longer worthy to be called your son. Treat me as one of your hired servants."' ²⁰And he arose and came to his father. But while he was still a long way off, his father saw him and felt compassion, and ran and embraced him and kissed him. ²¹And the son said to him, 'Father, I have sinned against heaven and before you. I am no longer worthy to be called your son.' ²²But the father said to his servants, 'Bring quickly the best robe, and put it on him, and put a ring on his hand, and shoes on his feet. ²³And bring the fattened calf and kill it, and let us eat and celebrate. ²⁴For this my son was dead, and is alive again; he was lost, and is found.' And they began to celebrate.

²⁵"Now his older son was in the field, and as he came and drew near to the house, he heard music and dancing.

²⁶And he called one of the servants and asked what these things meant. ²⁷And he said to him, 'Your brother has come, and your father has killed the fattened calf, because he has received him back safe and sound.' ²⁸But he was angry and refused to go in. His father came out and entreated him, ²⁹but he answered his father, 'Look, these many years I have served you, and I never disobeyed your command, yet you never gave me a young goat, that I might celebrate with my friends. ³⁰But when this son of yours came, who has devoured your property with prostitutes, you killed the fattened calf for him!' ³¹And he said to him, 'Son, you are always with me, and all that is mine is yours. ³²It was fitting to celebrate and be glad, for this your brother was dead, and is alive; he was lost, and is found.'"

S ometimes it seems like we spend a lot of time looking for things that are lost—lost keys, lost telephone numbers, a lost sock (it's always just one, never a pair). *Such a waste of time,* we think. *I could be doing something more useful.*

But in Luke 15 Jesus points out that God is in the lost-and-found business. He never considers it a waste of time. In fact, in His opinion, it's the most profitable activity He could pursue.

In this chapter, Jesus is responding to the grumblings of the scribes and Pharisees. The scribes were the "lawyers" of Jesus' day. They interpreted the law. The Pharisees applied these interpretations. They were far stricter than the other major religious sect of their day, the Sadducees. They maintained rigid standards of purity. This meant they not only avoided anything "unclean," but they also avoided those who didn't keep the same standards of purity they did.

On the top on their list of "unacceptable" people were the tax collectors and sinners. Tax collectors were not merely disliked; they were hated. As employees of the Roman government, it was easy for them to abuse their power and collect more taxes than were required. Corruption was common. Also, their association with the Romans who were Gentiles (non-Jews) made them religiously unclean. So, both for secular and religious reasons, tax collectors were the outcasts of Jewish society.

Sinners, on the other hand, were not necessarily bad people. They were the secularists of our day. They simply didn't pay much attention to all the religious rules and regulations. That was enough, however, to get them blackballed by the scribes and the Pharisees. So, it was to the shock and disgust of the religious leaders that Jesus was actually friendly toward these people and even ate with them.

It was that social climate that led Jesus to tell a series of parables with a two-fold purpose. They were, (1) aimed at the self-righteous attitude of the scribes and the Pharisees to show them how wrong they were. And at the same time, (2) the parables showed the others in His audience, the tax collectors and sinners, how greatly God valued them.

Each parable Jesus told had an increasingly more valuable item that was lost and then found. Jesus began with a sheep, then a silver coin, and finally a young man. Not only that, each time the percentage of loss was greater: one sheep in a hundred; one coin in ten; one son in two. And each time, the person who found the lost item rejoiced. In fact, not only did the finder rejoice, but he or she called in others to share the joy. The shepherd called in his friends and neighbors declaring, "Rejoice with me, for I have found my sheep that was lost" (Luke 15:6). The woman who lost the coin did the same exclaiming, "Rejoice with me, for I have found the coin that I had lost" (v. 9). And the father did even more: He threw a party. "For this my son was dead, and is alive again; he was lost and is found" (v. 24).

In direct contrast to the scornful attitude of the religious leaders toward those who were lost, Jesus showed them that God sees the lost as valuable. In fact, they are so valuable they're worth going to a lot of trouble to find. The shepherd left the 99 sheep and searched until he found the lost one. The woman lit a lamp, swept her house, and searched diligently until she found the lost coin. The father stood watch, looking longingly for his son to return—and when he did, the father killed the fattened calf for a feast.

What a comfort it was to the social rejects in the crowd to know that this was how God felt about them. In fact, Jesus declared, "Just so, I tell you, there is joy before the angels of God over one sinner who repents" (v. 10).

> *"When you look at the homeless, the prostitutes, the drug dealers, how do you feel? Is there a longing to bring them into God's kingdom?"*

These parables, however, also were convicting to the scribes and the Pharisees, especially as Jesus told the parable of the lost son. Unlike the other two, this story didn't end with finding the lost item. Instead Jesus brought in a second prodigal—the older son. This was a thinly disguised picture of the Pharisees. This older brother became angry at the celebration his father threw for his younger brother. In fact, the young man was so angry that he refused to come into the house and join in the joyful occasion. That was exactly what the scribes and the Pharisees would have done.

But how about you? When you look at the homeless, the prostitutes, the drug dealers, how do you feel? What comes to your mind about them? Is there a longing to bring them into God's kingdom? Or would you rather they just reaped what they have sown?

What about when someone who's wronged you repents and receives Christ? Do you continue to hold anger and bitterness toward them? While we may be glad that we don't fit the case of the younger son, we have to be careful we don't become the older brother either. He is the real prodigal son in this parable. He is the one, so far as we know, who never repented.

Go Deeper

A parable is a narrative that pairs an earthly story with a spiritual truth. The word *parable* means "to place alongside." Jesus' parables were spiritual truths that were expressed through everyday experiences. It was one of His most common ways to teach. More than one-third of Jesus' recorded teachings are in parable form.

Jesus used parables for two reasons. Parables were easy to remember because they were stories. Who can forget the story of the sower and his seed, the house built upon the sand or the father and his prodigal son?

In addition, Jesus used parables to keep His enemies off balance. Jesus needed time to teach His disciples. He wanted them to understand God's plan to bring people lost in sin to salvation. While the scribes and the Pharisees were often convinced a parable was directed at them, they couldn't prove it.

In Mark 4:11 Jesus told the disciples, "To you has been given the secret of the kingdom of God, but for those outside everything is in parables."

The parable of the sower, in Matthew 13:1–9, is an example of how Jesus used parables. When the disciples asked Him the reason for parables (Matt. 13:10), Christ told them it was so they could understand the mysteries of heaven (Matt. 13:11–16). Then He went on privately to explain the parable to them (Matt. 13:18–23). Through parables, He taught them (and us) important spiritual truths.

Express It

Train yourself to care for people in the same way Jesus cared for them. Is there someone who seems like an outcast in your workplace or church? Maybe he or she has been involved in "unacceptable" behaviors and has few friends. Maybe a mental health issue has caused them to be excluded from most circles. Maybe that person is just quiet and doesn't approach others easily. Begin praying every day for him or her. Make a special effort to talk with that person, smile at him or her, and treat that person with respect.

Consider It

As you read Luke 15:1–32, consider these questions:

1) Who is in the audience for these three parables? Do you see yourself in any of these groups?

_____

_____

_____

2) In the first two parables, what is lost? What happens when the lost is found?

_____

_____

_____

3) Put the familiar story of Luke 15:11–32 in your own words. Who is lost? Why? What brings the lost one home?

_____

_____

_____

4) How does the father respond? Why does he respond that way?

_____

_____

_____

5) As you consider this story, what do you think the older brother loses?

_____

_____

_____

6) What do you learn about what God values and what makes Him rejoice?

_____

_____

_____

7) How have you made God rejoice?

_____

_____

_____

Lesson
13

Money and Your Future

Whether it's possessions or actual coinage, wealth is an important topic in the teachings of Jesus. How we use it, or fail to use it, can make an eternal difference.

Luke 16:1–31

The Parable of the Dishonest Manager

16 He also said to the disciples, "There was a rich man who had a manager, and charges were brought to him that this man was wasting his possessions. ²And he called him and said to him, 'What is this that I hear about you? Turn in the account of your management, for you can no longer be manager.' ³And the manager said to himself, 'What shall I do, since my master is taking the management away from me? I am not strong enough to dig, and I am ashamed to beg. ⁴I have decided what to do, so that when I am removed from management, people may receive me into their houses.' ⁵So, summoning his master's debtors one by one, he said to the first, 'How much do you owe my master?' ⁶He said, 'A hundred measures of oil.' He said to him, 'Take your bill, and sit down quickly and write fifty.' ⁷Then he said to another, 'And how much do you owe?' He said, 'A hundred measures of wheat.' He said to him, 'Take your bill, and write eighty.' ⁸The master commended the dishonest manager for his shrewdness. For the sons of this world are more shrewd in dealing with their own generation than the sons of light. ⁹And I tell you, make friends for yourselves by means of unrighteous wealth, so that when it fails they may receive you into the eternal dwellings.

¹⁰"One who is faithful in a very little is also faithful in much, and one who is dishonest in a very little is also dishonest in much. ¹¹If then you have not been faithful in the unrighteous wealth, who will entrust to you the true riches? ¹²And if you have not been faithful in that which is another's, who will give you that which is your own? ¹³No servant can serve two masters, for either he will hate the one and love the other, or he will be devoted to the one and despise the other. You cannot serve God and money."

> # Key Verse
>
> *"And I tell you, make friends for yourselves by means of unrighteous wealth, so that when it fails they may receive you into the eternal dwellings"* (Luke 16:9).

The Law and the Kingdom of God

¹⁴The Pharisees, who were lovers of money, heard all these things, and they ridiculed him. ¹⁵And he said to them, "You are those who justify yourselves before men, but God knows your hearts. For what is exalted among men is an abomination in the sight of God.

¹⁶"The Law and the Prophets were until John; since then the good news of the kingdom of God is preached, and everyone forces his way into it. ¹⁷But it is easier for heaven and earth to pass away than for one dot of the Law to become void.

Divorce and Remarriage

¹⁸"Everyone who divorces his wife and marries another commits adultery, and he who marries a woman divorced from her husband commits adultery.

The Rich Man and Lazarus

¹⁹"There was a rich man who was clothed in purple and fine linen and who feasted sumptuously every day. ²⁰And at his gate was laid a poor man named Lazarus, covered with sores, ²¹who desired to be fed with what fell from the rich man's table. Moreover,

even the dogs came and licked his sores. ²²The poor man died and was carried by the angels to Abraham's side. The rich man also died and was buried, ²³and in Hades, being in torment, he lifted up his eyes and saw Abraham far off and Lazarus at his side. ²⁴And he called out, 'Father Abraham, have mercy on me, and send Lazarus to dip the end of his finger in water and cool my tongue, for I am in anguish in this flame.' ²⁵But Abraham said, 'Child, remember that you in your lifetime received your good things, and Lazarus in like manner bad things; but now he is comforted here, and you are in anguish. ²⁶And besides all this, between us and you a great chasm has been fixed, in order that those who would pass from here to you may not be able, and none may cross from there to us.' ²⁷And he said, 'Then I beg you, father, to send him to my father's house— ²⁸for I have five brothers—so that he may warn them, lest they also come into this place of torment.' ²⁹But Abraham said, 'They have Moses and the Prophets; let them hear them.' ³⁰And he said, 'No, father Abraham, but if someone goes to them from the dead, they will repent.' ³¹He said to him, 'If they do not hear Moses and the Prophets, neither will they be convinced if someone should rise from the dead.'"

***

The late Southern Baptist preacher, R. G. Lee, wrote that if people thought preachers talked too much about money, they should read their Bibles. Three of the Ten Commandments deal with possessions, sixteen of the thirty-eight parables Jesus told deal either with money or with stewardship and one verse out of every six in the Gospels discusses this topic.

Two of these parables on money are found in Luke 16. Both of them give us some important insights about the use of money and our future.

Some people find the parable of the dishonest steward (manager) difficult to understand. On the surface, it might seem like Jesus is saying it's OK to be dishonest. But He's not. Instead, He's showing His audience, who were basically religious people, that those who are not religious often know how to use their wealth more wisely than those who are. The parable of the dishonest manager is meant to teach us to use money shrewdly.

In this parable (16:1–9), Jesus tells about a rich man who had a manager who was accused of wasting his employer's possessions.

> ❝*If you've been blessed with a lot of possessions, good health, or tremendous talents, don't let that cause you to forget you are still a spiritual beggar.*❞

The employer demanded to see the books. The man knew it was just a matter of time, and he would be out of a job. He had to do something to prepare for the future. The idea of manual labor was out. He wasn't strong enough. The idea of begging was not appealing because he was too ashamed. So, he struck on another plan.

Acting shrewdly, he quickly called in his employer's debtors. When he found out what they owed, he lowered each person's bill by a large amount. That way, when he lost his job, he was hoping these people would be grateful enough to help him out in return.

While you can't buy your way into heaven, you can use your wealth to make sure that there's something waiting for you when you arrive. Jesus said, "Do not lay up for yourselves treasures on earth, where moth and rust destroy and where thieves break in and steal, but lay up for yourselves treasures in heaven, where neither moth nor rust destroys and where thieves do not break in and steal" (Matt. 6:19–20).

While Jesus was talking to His disciples, the Pharisees were listening in. And they didn't like what they heard. They ridiculed Jesus (Luke 16:14). So, Jesus told a second parable about a beggar named Lazarus and a rich man. This parable also looks to the future, not to show the wise use of money but to show the consequences of the misuse of money. Money can be used to store up treasures for the future or to bring condemnation for eternity. It all hinges on how we choose to use it.

The rich man remains unnamed in this parable, but the beggar is called Lazarus. This is not the Lazarus who is the brother of Mary and Martha and who Jesus raised from the dead. But this poor man laid outside the gates of the rich man's home hoping to be fed with the crumbs from his wealthy neighbor's table. Inside the rich man was clothed in expensive clothing and feasted lavishly every day.

But that changed when they died. Death is not the great equalizer; it's the great revealer. Death revealed that the rich man had lived only for his earthly enjoyment and paid the consequences. Lazarus, on the other hand, who had none of the world's wealth, received eternal comfort at "Abraham's side" (paradise).

Now Jesus wasn't saying that Lazarus went to heaven because he was a poor beggar and God felt sorry for him. While Jesus didn't feel the need to go into Lazarus' spiritual life, we know that only those who place their faith in Christ can see the Father (John 14:6).

But the story is a reminder that earthly wealth can take our attention away from spiritual truths. If we don't need anything physically here on earth, it's easy to forget that we are still spiritual beggars when it comes to God. Further on in the Gospel of Luke, Jesus says, "For it is easier for a camel to go through the eye of a needle than for a rich person to enter the kingdom of God" (Luke 18:25). Those who have no needs on earth easily forget they have enormous needs when it comes to heaven.

Consider what Jesus has given you not only in terms of money but also in terms of time and talents. Look to invest these gifts so you will have eternal rewards when you get to heaven. If you've been blessed with a lot of possessions, good health, or tremendous talents, don't let that cause you to forget you are still a spiritual beggar. If you haven't already, trust Christ as your Savior and make certain your eternal destination is heaven.

Go Deeper

Have you ever wondered why there were moneychangers in Israel at the time of Jesus? There were good reasons. Many different kinds of money were being used during those days. To make it more difficult, different coins were used for different purposes.

There were Roman coins. The most basic of these was the silver *denarius*. This was considered to be equal to the daily wage of a common laborer (Matt. 20:2). The *denarius* was the coin Jesus used when he told the Pharisees to "render to Caesar the things that are Caesar's, and to God the things that are God's" (Luke 20:21–26). There was also a copper coin (Greek, *assarion;* translated "penny" in the ESV) minted by the Romans. Five sparrows could be purchased for two *assarion* (Luke 12:6).

In addition, there were Greek coins. The basic Greek coin was the *drachma*. It was about the same as the Roman *denarius*. The "lost coin" in Jesus' parable (Luke 15:8–10) is called a *drachma*. Two-*drachma* coins were also minted by the Greeks. Jesus used one of these, found in the mouth of a fish, to pay the Temple taxes for Peter and Himself. *Four-drachma* pieces, called *a shekel,* were also used to pay Temple tax (Matt. 17:27). In Luke 19:11–27, Jesus speaks of another Greek coin, the *mina*. It equaled 100 *drachmas*.

Only one Jewish coin is mentioned in the New Testament. It is the *lepton* (ESV), (a "small copper coin") which was worth only a tiny fraction of a penny (Mark 12:41–44). It was all the widow had; yet she gave it to the Lord!

With so many coins, minted by so many governments, you can easily see why a moneychanger would have a thriving business changing money into the coins acceptable for use in the Jewish temple.

Express It

Think about how you use your time, money, and energy to make an eternal investment. Do you give to your church? Do you buy supplies and teach a Sunday school class? How about giving to a ministry that has blessed you? As much as possible track your gifts and measure the results.

Perhaps you can actually see a family sitting in church every week because you invited them once. If you teach Sunday school, learn where some of your past students are now. Is someone you once mentored now reaching others for Christ?

Thank God for each opportunity you have to make an eternal investment with the resources He's provided for you.

Consider It

As you read Luke 16:1–31, consider these questions:

1) Why was the manager fired?

_____

_____

_____

2) What does Jesus say about faithful stewardship?

_____

_____

_____

3) What happens to a divided heart?

_____

_____

_____

4) How does this passage (Luke 16:1–13) influence your perspective on wealth?

_____

_____

_____

5) What was life like for Lazarus before he died? After death?

_____

_____

_____

6) What was the rich man's first request? What was his second request?

_____

_____

_____

7) Have you ever tried to convince or warn someone about God's future plans? What happened?

_____

_____

_____

Signs of the Kingdom

A "kingdom" is any place where a king rules. Some day King Jesus will return and the whole world will be His kingdom. But for right now, Christ's kingdom is in the hearts of His followers. Wherever He rules in the lives of believers, that's where His kingdom is.

Read Luke 17:1–18:43

Luke 17:11–18:30

Jesus Cleanses Ten Lepers

17 ¹¹On the way to Jerusalem he was passing along between Samaria and Galilee. ¹²And as he entered a village, he was met by ten lepers, who stood at a distance ¹³and lifted up their voices, saying, "Jesus, Master, have mercy on us." ¹⁴When he saw them he said to them, "Go and show yourselves to the priests." And as they went they were cleansed. ¹⁵Then one of them, when he saw that he was healed, turned back, praising God with a loud voice; ¹⁶and he fell on his face at Jesus' feet, giving him thanks. Now he was a Samaritan. ¹⁷Then Jesus answered, "Were not ten cleansed? Where are the nine? ¹⁸Was no one found to return and give praise to God except this foreigner?" ¹⁹And he said to him, "Rise and go your way; your faith has made you well."

The Coming of the Kingdom

²⁰Being asked by the Pharisees when the kingdom of God would come, he answered them, "The kingdom of God is not coming with signs to be observed, ²¹nor will they say, 'Look, here it is!'or 'There!' for behold, the kingdom of God is in the midst of you."

²²And he said to the disciples, "The days are coming when you will desire to see one of the days of the Son of Man, and you will not see it. ²³And they will say to you, 'Look, there!'or 'Look, here!' Do not go out or follow them. ²⁴For as the lightning flashes and lights up the sky from one side to the other, so will the Son of Man be in his day. ²⁵But first he must suffer many things and be rejected by this generation. ²⁶Just as it was in the days of Noah, so will it be in the days of the Son of Man. ²⁷They were eating and drinking and marrying and being given in marriage, until the day when Noah entered the ark, and the flood came

> # Key Verse
>
> *Being asked by the Pharisees when the kingdom of God would come, he answered them, "The kingdom of God is not coming with signs to be observed, nor will they say, 'Look, here it is!' or 'There!' for behold, the kingdom of God is in the midst of you"* (Luke 17:20–21).

and destroyed them all. ²⁸Likewise, just as it was in the days of Lot—they were eating and drinking, buying and selling, planting and building, ²⁹but on the day when Lot went out from Sodom, fire and sulfur rained from heaven and destroyed them all— ³⁰so will it be on the day when the Son of Man is revealed. ³¹On that day, let the one who is on the housetop, with his goods in the house, not come down to take them away, and likewise let the one who is in the field not turn back. ³²Remember Lot's wife. ³³Whoever seeks to preserve his life will lose it, but whoever loses his life will keep it. ³⁴I tell you, in that night there will be two in one bed. One will be taken and the other left. ³⁵There will be two women grinding together. One will be taken and the other left."* ³⁷And they said to him, "Where, Lord?" He said to them, "Where the corpse is, there the vultures will gather."

The Parable of the Persistent Widow

18 And he told them a parable to the effect that they ought always to pray and

*36: Some manuscripts add verse 36: Two men will be in the field; one will be taken and the other left.

not lose heart. [2]He said, "In a certain city there was a judge who neither feared God nor respected man. [3]And there was a widow in that city who kept coming to him and saying, 'Give me justice against my adversary.' [4]For a while he refused, but afterward he said to himself, 'Though I neither fear God nor respect man, [5]yet because this widow keeps bothering me, I will give her justice, so that she will not beat me down by her continual coming.'" [6]And the Lord said, "Hear what the unrighteous judge says. [7]And will not God give justice to his elect, who cry to him day and night? Will he delay long over them? [8]I tell you, he will give justice to them speedily. Nevertheless, when the Son of Man comes, will he find faith on earth?"

The Pharisee and the Tax Collector

[9]He also told this parable to some who trusted in themselves that they were righteous, and treated others with contempt: [10]"Two men went up into the temple to pray, one a Pharisee and the other a tax collector. [11]The Pharisee, standing by himself, prayed thus: 'God, I thank you that I am not like other men, extortioners, unjust, adulterers, or even like this tax collector. [12]I fast twice a week; I give tithes of all that I get.' [13]But the tax collector, standing far off, would not even lift up his eyes to heaven, but beat his breast, saying, 'God, be merciful to me, a sinner!' [14]I tell you, this man went down to his house justified, rather than the other. For everyone who exalts himself will be humbled, but the one who humbles himself will be exalted."

Let the Children Come to Me

[15]Now they were bringing even infants to him that he might touch them. And when the disciples saw it, they rebuked them. [16]But Jesus called them to him, saying, "Let the children come to me, and do not hinder them, for to such belongs the kingdom of God. [17]Truly, I say to you, whoever does not receive the kingdom of God like a child shall not enter it."

The Rich Ruler

[18]And a ruler asked him, "Good Teacher, what must I do to inherit eternal life?" [19]And Jesus said to him, "Why do you call me good? No one is good except God alone. [20]You know the commandments: 'Do not commit adultery, Do not murder, Do not steal, Do not bear false witness, Honor your father and mother.'" [21]And he said, "All these I have kept from my youth." [22]When Jesus heard this, he said to him, "One thing you still lack. Sell all that you have and distribute to the poor, and you will have treasure in heaven; and come, follow me." [23]But when he heard these things, he became very sad, for he was extremely rich. [24]Jesus, seeing that he had become sad, said, "How difficult it is for those who have wealth to enter the kingdom of God! [25]For it is easier for a camel to go through the eye of a needle than for a rich person to enter the kingdom of God." [26]Those who heard it said, "Then who can be saved?" [27]But he said, "What is impossible with men is possible with God." [28]And Peter said, "See, we have left our homes and followed you." [29]And he said to them, "Truly, I say to you, there is no one who has left house or wife or brothers or parents or children, for the sake of the kingdom of God, [30]who will not receive many times more in this time, and in the age to come eternal life."

As He was traveling to Jerusalem, a group of Pharisees approached Jesus and wanted to know when the kingdom of God would come (Luke 17:20–37). Jesus' answer probably surprised them. The Pharisees, like most of the Jews in that day, were expecting God to send a Messiah who would overthrow the Roman government. He would then set up His own kingdom on earth. And if that were the case, and if Jesus was that Messiah, they thought there ought to be some sign that this was about to happen.

But Jesus answered, "The kingdom of God is not coming with signs to be observed." In other words, at this point, it was not going to be an outward, observable kingdom. Jesus didn't say that the kingdom wasn't coming; it just wasn't going to be the kind of physical kingdom that these religious leaders were expecting.

When the physical kingdom would come, Jesus assured them, everyone would know it. "For as the lightning flashes and lights up the sky from one side to the other, so will the Son of Man be in his day" (17:24). But that day was not yet. For now, the King would be establishing His kingdom in the hearts of His followers. Instead of an outward kingdom with banners and armies and all the other trappings, it was going to be with signs that were not physically visible. But there would still be signs, so what would they be?

One sign that the kingdom has been established in a person's heart is gratitude. Jesus healed ten lepers and told them to go show themselves to the priests. As they went, all ten were cleansed, but only one turned back to express gratitude. To that one, Jesus said, "Rise and go your way; your faith has made you well." The ten lepers were cured physically as they left Jesus (17:14), but the one with the grateful heart was cured spiritually (17:19). God's kingdom was set up in his heart.

Gratitude is always an indication that the King is in residence. The apostle Paul said, "Give thanks in all circumstances; for this is the will of God in Christ Jesus for you" (1 Thess. 5:18). "All circumstances" means the bad times as well the good. When the kingdom dwells in you, all things are worthy of gratitude.

> **"The King's priorities are different from the world's. When His kingdom is established in your heart, yours will be too."**

Another sign is humility. Jesus told the parable of the Pharisee and the tax collector (Luke 18:9–14). Both went to the temple. The Pharisee, prayed, "God, I thank you that I am not like other men, extortioners, unjust, adulterers, or even like this tax collector. I fast twice a week; I give tithes of all that I get." How proud that Pharisee was of himself. The tax collector, however, did not consider himself worthy but beat his breast (a sign of mourning) and cried out, "God, be merciful to me, a sinner!" It's pretty obvious who had the kingdom dwelling in his heart.

Furthermore, the kingdom dwells in those who are child-like (18:15–17). Child-like is not the same as childish. *Childish* means "immature," "selfish," "self-centered." That's definitely not a sign of the kingdom. Instead, *child-like* means "trusting." When you're lost, confused, and don't know what to do, you trust the King. That's a sign the kingdom is in you.

And then there is the indicator of priorities. When your priorities change, it is a sure sign that the King has set up His kingdom in your heart. At the top of the world's list of priorities is wealth. A rich young ruler asked Jesus, "Good Teacher, what must I do to inherit eternal life?" Jesus said to him, "Why do you call me good? No one is good except God alone. You know the commandments, 'Do not commit adultery, Do not murder, Do not steal, Do not bear false witness, Honor your father and mother.'" The ruler replied, "All these I have kept from my youth." The chances this young man was being totally honest are slim. Giving him the benefit of the doubt, however, Jesus added one more thing to the list. "One thing you still lack. Sell all that you have and distribute to the poor, and you will have treasure in heaven; and come, follow me" (18:18–30). Jesus was asking him to turn his priorities upside down. And the young man couldn't do it.

The King's priorities are different from the world's. When His kingdom is established in your heart, yours will be too.

When we pray the Lord's Prayer, we plead, "Your kingdom come." That's Christ's future physical kingdom. His spiritual kingdom is already here—just look for the signs.

Go Deeper

As you study Luke's Gospel, watch for Jesus' work and words that point to Him as prophet (proclaiming the Word of God), priest (mediating between God and man), and king (exercising His right to rule over all).

- Prophet: God promised Moses that He would send Israel a great prophet (Deut. 18:15–18). Jesus Christ fulfilled that promise as Peter says in Acts 3:22: "Moses said, 'The Lord God will raise up for you a prophet like me from your brothers. You shall listen to him in whatever he tells you.'"

- Priest: Psalm 110:4 speaks prophetically of a "priest forever after the order of Melchizedek." Jesus also fulfilled that office as the writer testifies in Hebrews 4:14–16, saying:

"Since then we have a great high priest who has passed through the heavens, Jesus, the Son of God, let us hold fast our confession."

- King: The Magi came to Jerusalem looking for a king. They asked, "Where is he who has been born king of the Jews?" (Matt. 2:2). Jesus was the fulfillment of an Old Testament prophecy in Micah 5:2 which promised a ruler to be born in Bethlehem.

The religious leaders of Jesus' day didn't understand there weren't several people coming to fulfill these roles. But in fact, all these persons would be rolled up into one—Jesus Christ.

Express It

Following are the signs indicating that the kingdom has been established in your life (featured in the devotional study for Luke 17–18). Take time to reflect on each sign individually and complete the following exercises.

Gratitude—Today write God a poem or a note thanking Him for something you're grateful for.

Humility—List the qualities of those people you would call truly humble.

Child-like—Read Psalm 91 and write especially meaningful verses on an index card to keep beside your bed. Read these verses every morning and evening when you feel lost and confused, and you're struggling to trust the Lord.

Changed priorities—Relate to a Christian friend a recent experience that displayed to you just how much your priorities have changed since you began following Christ.

Consider It

As you read Luke 17:1–18:43, consider these questions:

1) What happened when Jesus healed the ten lepers?

2) Why is it significant that the grateful man was a Samaritan?

3) Toward whom was the parable of the tax collector and the Pharisee directed? Which man went away justified? Why?

4) Why do you think the disciples rebuked the parents in Luke 18:15?

5) Explain in your own words how you receive the kingdom of God.

6) Why would it be difficult for the wealthy to enter the kingdom? Is it possible at all?

7) In what ways does your life show that the kingdom lives in you?

Lesson 15

From Jericho to Jerusalem

The end was quickly approaching. Within just a few days, the religious leaders would have their way—and Jesus would be crucified. But before that happened, Jesus had some important truths to teach His disciples, as well as you and me.

Read Luke 19:1–20:47

Luke 19:1–48

Jesus and Zacchaeus

19 He entered Jericho and was passing through. ²And there was a man named Zacchaeus. He was a chief tax collector and was rich. ³And he was seeking to see who Jesus was, but on account of the crowd he could not, because he was small of stature. ⁴So he ran on ahead and climbed up into a sycamore tree to see him, for he was about to pass that way. ⁵And when Jesus came to the place, he looked up and said to him, "Zacchaeus, hurry and come down, for I must stay at your house today." ⁶So he hurried and came down and received him joyfully. ⁷And when they saw it, they all grumbled, "He has gone in to be the guest of a man who is a sinner." ⁸And Zacchaeus stood and said to the Lord, "Behold, Lord, the half of my goods I give to the poor. And if I have defrauded anyone of anything, I restore it fourfold." ⁹And Jesus said to him, "Today salvation has come to this house, since he also is a son of Abraham. ¹⁰For the Son of Man came to seek and to save the lost."

The Parable of the Ten Minas

¹¹As they heard these things, he proceeded to tell a parable, because he was near to Jerusalem, and because they supposed that the kingdom of God was to appear immediately. ¹²He said therefore, "A nobleman went into a far country to receive for himself a kingdom and then return. ¹³Calling ten of his servants, he gave them ten minas, and said to them, 'Engage in business until I come.' ¹⁴But his citizens hated him and sent a delegation after him, saying, 'We do not want this man to reign over us.' ¹⁵When he returned, having received the kingdom, he ordered these servants to whom he had given the money to be called to him, that he might know what they had gained by doing business. ¹⁶The first came before him, saying, 'Lord, your

> # Key Verse
>
> And he was teaching daily in the temple. The chief priests and the scribes and the principal men of the people were seeking to destroy him, but they did not find anything they could do, for all the people were hanging on his words (Luke 19:47–48).

mina has made ten minas more.' ¹⁷And he said to him, 'Well done, good servant! Because you have been faithful in a very little, you shall have authority over ten cities.' ¹⁸And the second came, saying, 'Lord, your mina has made five minas.' ¹⁹And he said to him, 'And you are to be over five cities.' ²⁰Then another came, saying, 'Lord, here is your mina, which I kept laid away in a handkerchief; ²¹for I was afraid of you, because you are a severe man. You take what you did not deposit, and reap what you did not sow.' ²²He said to him, 'I will condemn you with your own words, you wicked servant! You knew that I was a severe man, taking what I did not deposit and reaping what I did not sow? ²³Why then did you not put my money in the bank, and at my coming I might have collected it with interest?' ²⁴And he said to those who stood by, 'Take the mina from him, and give it to the one who has the ten minas.' ²⁵And they said to him, 'Lord, he has ten minas!' ²⁶'I tell you that to everyone who has, more will be given, but from the one who has not, even what he has will be taken away. ²⁷But as for these enemies of mine, who did not want me to reign over them, bring them here and slaughter them before me.'"

The Triumphal Entry

²⁸And when he had said these things, he went on ahead, going up to Jerusalem. ²⁹When he drew near to Bethphage and Bethany, at the mount that is called Olivet, he sent two of the disciples, ³⁰saying, "Go into the village in front of you, where on entering you will find a colt tied, on which no one has ever yet sat. Untie it and bring it here. ³¹If anyone asks you, 'Why are you untying it?' you shall say this: 'The Lord has need of it.'" ³²So those who were sent went away and found it just as he had told them. ³³And as they were untying the colt, its owners said to them, "Why are you untying the colt?" ³⁴And they said, "The Lord has need of it." ³⁵And they brought it to Jesus, and throwing their cloaks on the colt, they set Jesus on it. ³⁶And as he rode along, they spread their cloaks on the road. ³⁷As he was drawing near—already on the way down the Mount of Olives—the whole multitude of his disciples began to rejoice and praise God with a loud voice for all the mighty works that they had seen, ³⁸saying, "Blessed is the King who comes in the name of the Lord! Peace in heaven and glory in the highest!" ³⁹And some of the Pharisees in the crowd said to him, "Teacher, rebuke your disciples." ⁴⁰He answered, "I tell you, if these were silent, the very stones would cry out."

Jesus Weeps over Jerusalem

⁴¹And when he drew near and saw the city, he wept over it, ⁴²saying, "Would that you, even you, had known on this day the things that make for peace! But now they are hidden from your eyes. ⁴³For the days will come upon you, when your enemies will set up a barricade around you and surround you and hem you in on every side ⁴⁴and tear you down to the ground, you and your children within you. And they will not leave one stone upon another in you, because you did not know the time of your visitation."

Jesus Cleanses the Temple

⁴⁵And he entered the temple and began to drive out those who sold, ⁴⁶saying to them, "It is written, 'My house shall be a house of prayer,' but you have made it a den of robbers."

⁴⁷And he was teaching daily in the temple. The chief priests and the scribes and the principal men of the people were seeking to destroy him, ⁴⁸but they did not find anything they could do, for all the people were hanging on his words.

A s the end drew near, Jesus was on the final leg of His journey. The distance from Jericho to Jerusalem was about 17 miles. But in that short distance, a great many important events took place.

First, Jesus encountered a tax collector named Zacchaeus. Zacchaeus was short on height but long on *chutzpah* (nerve). He was determined to see Jesus even if it was from the rather undignified perch of a Sycamore tree. Jesus, seeing the man's sincerity, called to him: "Zacchaeus, hurry and come down, for I must stay at your house today" (Luke 19:5). Of course, that didn't set well with everyone else. Zacchaeus was a "chief tax collector and was rich." Neither of those would earn him any popularity points. (Remember from an earlier lesson that tax collectors got rich by abusing their power and collecting more tax than necessary.)

But, when Zacchaeus met Jesus, his life changed completely. He declared he would give half his wealth to the poor. Not only that, he would restore four-fold anything he had taken dishonestly. Jesus' response was, "Today salvation has come to this house."

A real encounter with Jesus is a life-changing experience. The apostle Paul says, "Therefore, if anyone is in Christ, he is a new creation. The old has passed away; behold, the new has come" (2 Cor. 5:17). Has Jesus changed your life?

Jesus then told a parable about a nobleman. This man went away to a "far country" to get permission to be king over his homeland. He left ten of his servants behind, gave them each a *mina* (about three months' wages) and instructed them to do business for him while he was gone. After he left, some of the citizens of his homeland sent a delegation to the far country to object to his rule over them. Their objection was dismissed. When the nobleman returned, he rewarded those who were given the *minas* according to how faithfully they used his resources. Those who didn't want him to be king over them were put to death.

If we examine additional passages in Scripture, we discover that in the parable of the ten *minas* Jesus was telling listeners that their will be two future judgments: the Judgment Seat of Christ where believers will be judged according to their faithfulness (2 Cor. 5:10), and the Great White Throne Judgment for those who rejected Him as their Savior (Rev. 20:11–15). Ultimately, everyone faces judgment. Knowing that, we need to be ready. For Christians, it means evaluating how we are using the resources God gives us. For the unbeliever, it means submitting his or her life to Christ and asking Him to save them. How foolish it would be to know what's coming but not prepare for it.

"You should feel free to bring your questions to God's Word and seek an answer—that's how we grow spiritually."

In Luke 19:28–30, Jesus was preparing to enter the city; He sent two of His disciples ahead to bring back a colt for Him to ride on. Jesus went to great lengths to make it clear this was no ordinary entrance. Zechariah 9:9 prophesies that Israel's king would enter riding on "a colt, the foal of a donkey." Jesus made it clear this prophecy was being fulfilled. Yet He knew it wouldn't make any difference. Jerusalem's destiny was set; destruction was ahead and He wept over it.

Triumphantly, however, Jesus came into the city. The journey was over and His final days had arrived. For a second time, He entered the temple and cleansed it. The apostle John tells us Jesus took this same action at the beginning of His ministry (John 2:13–17). In a short time, however, corruption had crept back. When it comes to sin, we can never let down our guard. If we think we've dealt with something once and for all, we're only fooling ourselves.

Jesus' presence in the city solidified the decision of the religious leaders to get rid of Him. In their efforts, a series of encounters occurred which left the chief priests and scribes defeated but defiant.

First they asked Jesus where His authority came from. He turned that around by asking where John the Baptist's authority came from. The religious leaders knew that was a no-win question, so they refused to answer.

Then Jesus told a parable about some wicked tenants. These tenants rented a vineyard but refused to pay the rent. When the owner sent his servants to collect what was due him, they abused them and sent them away empty handed. Finally the owner sent his son. The renters not only abused him but actually killed him. Jesus concluded with a serious warning: "What then will the owner of the vineyard do to them? He will come and destroy those tenants and give the vineyard to others" (Luke 20:15–16).

Even the Sadducees (another group of religious leaders) tried their hand at tricking Jesus. Unlike the Pharisees, the Sadducees represented the more liberal side of Judaism. They didn't believe in the immortality of the soul or in the resurrection of the dead. So, they proposed a ridiculous situation (a woman marrying seven brothers, one at a time). They asked Jesus for a judgment. As usual, Jesus went to the heart of the issue: there is no marriage in heaven. Furthermore, God is not the God of the dead—so there has to be a resurrection. Case closed! It's no wonder "they no longer dared to ask him any question" (20:40).

Jesus never discouraged honest seekers, but He had no time for those with hidden agendas. You should feel free to bring your questions to God's Word and seek an answer—that's how we grow spiritually. But be careful about looking for proofs to simply support your arguments. The Bible is bread for daily living, not cake for special occasions.

Go Deeper

Some say that Jesus cleansed the temple only once. They believe the apostle John simply moved the time to the early part of Jesus' ministry. It is more likely, however, Jesus cleansed the temple twice. The first time was in the beginning stages of His earthly ministry. On that occasion, He told Israel's leaders to stop misusing God's holy dwelling-place (John 2:13–17). The second time was shortly after His final entry into Jerusalem (Luke 19:45–46). Christ used the second time to tell the Jews that their worship was corrupted. It was not acceptable to God. Mark 11:17 says, "And he [Jesus] was teaching them and saying to them, 'Is it not written, "My house shall be called a house of prayer for all nations"? But you have made it a den of robbers.'" He was actually quoting from Isaiah 56:7 and Jeremiah 7:11.

He warned as well that the rejection of their Messiah would bring disaster upon them. "The stone that the builders rejected has become the cornerstone" (Luke 20:17). But they didn't listen.

What made it worse, the money-changers set up their tables in the temple area known as the "Court of the Gentiles." It was the only place where non-Jewish worshippers were allowed to worship the true God. Isaiah 56 tells us God intended to extend His blessings to these people as well as the nation of Israel. Jesus demonstrated that by limiting the Gentiles to only one small area in the temple, the Jewish leaders failed to be a kingdom of priests to all nations. (See Ex. 19:5–6.) And to use that area to sell their products was an even greater failure.

Express It

Have you ever used the Bible as piece of cake rather than bread, reading it occasionally to prove a point instead of taking in a daily diet of the Word to help you grow more like Jesus? It's important for you as a Christian to have the spiritual food the Bible offers you on a daily basis. Start today. Make a daily Bible reading menu plan for next month. On your calendar, note what portion of God's Word you'll read each day. Maybe you want to read a specific book of the Bible or you may want to choose a topic and read a number of verses on that topic each day—note them on your calendar and then work your plan. You'll find the nourishment well worth the effort.

Consider It

As you read Luke 19:1–20:47, consider these questions:

1) What do we learn about Jesus' mission statement from the story of Zacchaeus?

_____

_____

_____

2) How have you seen Him accomplish this so far in Luke?

_____

_____

_____

3) In the parable of the ten *minas,* what do we learn about the master's expectations?

_____

_____

_____

4) In your own words, describe what the servants did and the master's response.

_____

_____

_____

5) What does this parable say about your part in the kingdom of God?

_____

_____

_____

6) What does Jesus predict for Jerusalem's future? Why?

_____

_____

_____

7) Why did the religious leaders decide not to ask Jesus any more questions? How does this apply to you?

_____

_____

_____

Darkest Before the Dawn

Are you concerned about the events happening in the world? Many people are. But Jesus said when circumstances look their worst, the best is not far off. Don't look around, look up. Jesus is coming soon.

Luke 21:1–38

The Widow's Offering

21 Jesus looked up and saw the rich putting their gifts into the offering box, [2]and he saw a poor widow put in two small copper coins. [3]And he said, "Truly, I tell you, this poor widow has put in more than all of them. [4]For they all contributed out of their abundance, but she out of her poverty put in all she had to live on."

Jesus Foretells Destruction of the Temple

[5]And while some were speaking of the temple, how it was adorned with noble stones and offerings, he said, [6]"As for these things that you see, the days will come when there will not be left here one stone upon another that will not be thrown down." [7]And they asked him, "Teacher, when will these things be, and what will be the sign when these things are about to take place?" [8]And he said, "See that you are not led astray. For many will come in my name, saying, 'I am he!' and, 'The time is at hand!' Do not go after them. [9]And when you hear of wars and tumults, do not be terrified, for these things must first take place, but the end will not be at once."

Jesus Foretells Wars and Persecution

[10]Then he said to them, "Nation will rise against nation, and kingdom against kingdom. [11]There will be great earthquakes, and in various places famines and pestilences. And there will be terrors and great signs from heaven. [12]But before all this they will lay their hands on you and persecute you, delivering you up to the synagogues and prisons, and you will be brought before kings and governors for my name's sake. [13]This will be your opportunity to bear witness. [14]Settle it therefore in your minds not to meditate beforehand how to answer, [15]for I will give you a mouth and wisdom, which none of your

> # Key Verse
> "And when you hear of wars and tumults, do not be terrified, for these things must first take place, but the end will not be at once" (Luke 21:9).

adversaries will be able to withstand or contradict. [16]You will be delivered up even by parents and brothers and relatives and friends, and some of you they will put to death. [17]You will be hated by all for my name's sake. [18]But not a hair of your head will perish. [19]By your endurance you will gain your lives.

Jesus Foretells Destruction of Jerusalem

[20]"But when you see Jerusalem surrounded by armies, then know that its desolation has come near. [21]Then let those who are in Judea flee to the mountains, and let those who are inside the city depart, and let not those who are out in the country enter it, [22]for these are days of vengeance, to fulfill all that is written. [23]Alas for women who are pregnant and for those who are nursing infants in those days! For there will be great distress upon the earth and wrath against this people. [24]They will fall by the edge of the sword and be led captive among all nations, and Jerusalem will be trampled underfoot by the Gentiles, until the times of the Gentiles are fulfilled.

The Coming of the Son of Man

[25]"And there will be signs in sun and moon and stars, and on the earth distress of nations in perplexity because

of the roaring of the sea and the waves, [26]people fainting with fear and with foreboding of what is coming on the world. For the powers of the heavens will be shaken. [27]And then they will see the Son of Man coming in a cloud with power and great glory. [28]Now when these things begin to take place, straighten up and raise your heads, because your redemption is drawing near."

The Lesson of the Fig Tree

[29]And he told them a parable: "Look at the fig tree, and all the trees. [30]As soon as they come out in leaf, you see for yourselves and know that the summer is already near. [31]So also, when you see these things taking place, you know that the kingdom of God is near. [32]Truly, I say to you, this generation will not pass away until all has taken place. [33]Heaven and earth will pass away, but my words will not pass away.

Watch Yourselves

[34]"But watch yourselves lest your hearts be weighed down with dissipation and drunkenness and cares of this life, and that day come upon you suddenly like a trap. [35]For it will come upon all who dwell on the face of the whole earth. [36]But stay awake at all times, praying that you may have strength to escape all these things that are going to take place, and to stand before the Son of Man."

[37]And every day he was teaching in the temple, but at night he went out and lodged on the mount called Olivet. [38]And early in the morning all the people came to him in the temple to hear him.

Woody Allen said, "Mankind is caught at a crossroads. One road leads to hopelessness and despair, while the other leads to total annihilation. Let us pray we have the wisdom to choose rightly." But there is a third option that probably never entered Woody Allen's mind—the return of Christ.

That's not to say there won't be turmoil and destruction. Jesus predicted that the temple would be destroyed (Luke 21:5–6) and Jerusalem wiped out (vv. 20–24). This took place in A.D. 70 when the Roman armies led by Titus Vespasianus (who later became the emperor of Rome) burned the temple and tore down the city's walls. Not one stone was left standing on another as Jesus foretold, except for a portion of the western wall.

According to Jesus, the Jews would "fall by the edge of the sword and be led captive among all nations, and Jerusalem will be trampled underfoot by the Gentiles, until the times of the Gentiles are fulfilled" (v. 24).

And these tribulations would not be confined just to the nation of Israel. "Nation will rise against nation, and kingdom against kingdom" (v. 10). It will be worldwide. Even nature will enter into the battle with great earthquakes, famines and pestilence (v. 11).

In addition, Jesus said the heavens themselves will give warning. There will be signs in the "sun and moon and stars." This kind of disruption in the solar system will affect the tides of the ocean and the sea and waves will roar (v. 25).

While some of these things have occurred in the past, the intensity will increase as the time for Christ's return draws near. In fact, Revelation 6:8 declares that a fourth of the human race will be destroyed "with sword and with famine and with pestilence and by wild beasts of the earth." Another third is destroyed by a vast supernaturally empowered army led by four fallen angels released from the river Euphrates for that purpose (Rev. 9:15,18). So, by the time Christ returns in power and great glory at the end of the Tribulation, over half the world's population (currently estimated at nearly 7 billion) will be destroyed. Such devastation has never been seen.

In addition, every person's hand will be against those who choose to follow Christ. Jesus warns, "You will be delivered up even by parents and brothers and relatives and friends, and some of you they will put to death. You will be hated by all for my name's sake" (Luke 21:16–17). Again this is something that has gone on from the beginning of time. Cain killed Abel because Abel was more righteous than he was. All the apostles, except for John, met a martyr's death. It is claimed that more people were killed for Christ during the 20th century than all the other previous centuries combined.

But Jesus said this will get even worse. For those who choose to follow Him during the time of the Antichrist (the Tribulation), the persecution will be intense. Yet many will make that sacrifice. Revelation 7:9 says, "After this I looked, and behold, a great multitude that no one could number, from every nation, from all tribes and peoples and languages, standing before the throne and before the Lamb, clothed in white robes, with palm branches in their hands." The question is asked: "Who are these?" The answer given: "These are the ones coming out of the great tribulation" (Rev. 7:13–14).

> *"Just as it is darkest before the dawn, so the more evil our world becomes, the stronger the indicator Christ is coming soon."*

While those who have heard the Gospel and rejected it will be misled (2 Thess. 2:11), multitudes will embrace the Savior even if it means losing their lives. Trading a few earthly years for the riches of eternity will make it worthwhile.

While most would consider these as desperate and discouraging times, Jesus saw it differently. He said, "Now when these things begin to take place, straighten up and raise your heads, because your redemption is drawing near" (Luke 21:28). How could He say that?

Just as it is darkest before the dawn, so the more evil our world becomes, the stronger the indicator Christ is coming soon. Jesus will not allow wickedness to continue forever. His army is ready in heaven (Rev. 19:11–14), and at the right time evil will be destroyed and there will be a new heaven and a new earth. But mankind will be allowed to do its worst before Jesus does His best.

While it's true that the Church will not have to go through the Tribulation (see Go Deeper), that doesn't mean we won't experience hard times. Sometimes those hard times will be directly related to our relationship with Jesus. Our coworkers and even our family may reject us because we're "Christians." Other times the moral principles and values we hold because of our faith in Christ will put us in direct conflict with society around us. And as our society turns its back on the Bible, unfortunately, you can expect more of that.

But take courage—Jesus is drawing near. The time is close when we will be taken home to be with Him. No more tears, no more sorrows—just a never-ending joy in our Savior's presence.

Go Deeper

The study part of this lesson indicated that the Church would not experience the Tribulation. Perhaps you've heard of an event called "the Rapture." The word *Rapture* is not found in the Bible. It comes from the Latin word meaning "to snatch away" and was coined to describe that time when the Church is caught up to meet the Lord in the air. Scripture says Jesus is coming for His Church. He will take His people to be with Him. The apostle Paul describes this event in 1 Thessalonians 4:13–17.

Although not everyone agrees when the Rapture will occur, I believe the Rapture will happen before the Tribulation (the time when the Antichrist rules). Here's why:

• The verses that tell us to watch for the Lord's coming to remove the Church do not tell us to watch for the Tribulation first (1 Thess. 5:1–11; Titus 2:13).

• The Tribulation will involve Israel and the world but not the church.

• The Church is not destined for God's wrath but for salvation (1 Thess. 5:9; 2 Pet. 2:9).

• Believers will be saved from the wrath to come (Rom. 1:18; 5:9; 1 Thess. 1:10).

• The Lord has committed Himself to keep the Church from the hour of Tribulation (Rev. 3:10).

Whether we agree on the timing of the Rapture or not, one thing is sure: Jesus is coming again and for that we can rejoice. The only way out of the mess we've made of this world may be up.

Express It

When you think about Jesus' return, how do you feel? Fearful because of the unknown? Fearful because you're unsure of your salvation? Or excited that you'll see your Savior and King come back to Earth?

If you're fearful of the unknown, determine today to search the Bible for all information concerning the coming of Christ. Try passages like these: Matthew 24–25; Mark 13:32–37; Acts 1:10–11; 1 Thessalonians 4:13–18; 2 Thessalonians 2; 1 John 3:2.

If you're fearful because you're unsure of your salvation, receive Jesus into your life today and begin attending a Bible-believing church. Begin reading your Bible consistently, make Christian friends, and listen to good Bible teaching on radio and television.

Excited about Christ's return? Take a moment to rejoice that you know the Savior and that His coming is a day you are eager to experience.

Consider It

As you read Luke 21:1–38, consider these questions:

1) What is Jesus' warning to those who seek signs?

_____

_____

_____

2) What will happen to Jesus' followers?

_____

_____

_____

3) What opportunities do Jesus' followers have during this time?

_____

_____

_____

4) What will Jesus do for those who have these opportunities?

_____

_____

_____

5) What can we expect to lose and to gain?

_____

_____

_____

6) Make a list of what you can do to prepare for Christ's return.

_____

_____

_____

7) How does this passage help you face the future?

_____

_____

_____

Lesson 17

The Blessings of Forgiveness

No one has suffered more wrong than Jesus. Betrayed by one in his innermost circle of disciples; deserted by all who called Him friend; the victim of injustice committed by Jew and Gentile alike. Yet His response was, "Father, forgive them."

Read Luke 22:1–23:56

Luke 22:14–71

Institution of the Lord's Supper

22 ¹⁴And when the hour came, he reclined at table, and the apostles with him. ¹⁵And he said to them, "I have earnestly desired to eat this Passover with you before I suffer. ¹⁶For I tell you I will not eat it until it is fulfilled in the kingdom of God." ¹⁷And he took a cup, and when he had given thanks he said, "Take this, and divide it among yourselves. ¹⁸For I tell you that from now on I will not drink of the fruit of the vine until the kingdom of God comes." ¹⁹And he took bread, and when he had given thanks, he broke it and gave it to them, saying, "This is my body, which is given for you. Do this in remembrance of me." ²⁰And likewise the cup after they had eaten, saying, "This cup that is poured out for you is the new covenant in my blood. ²¹But behold, the hand of him who betrays me is with me on the table. ²²For the Son of Man goes as it has been determined, but woe to that man by whom he is betrayed!" ²³And they began to question one another, which of them it could be who was going to do this.

Who Is the Greatest?

²⁴A dispute also arose among them, as to which of them was to be regarded as the greatest. ²⁵And he said to them, "The kings of the Gentiles exercise lordship over them, and those in authority over them are called benefactors. ²⁶But not so with you. Rather, let the greatest among you become as the youngest, and the leader as one who serves. ²⁷For who is the greater, one who reclines at table or one who serves? Is it not the one who reclines at table? But I am among you as the one who serves.

²⁸"You are those who have stayed with me in my trials, ²⁹and I assign to you, as my Father assigned to me, a kingdom, ³⁰that you may eat and drink at my table

> ## Key Verse
>
> And Jesus said, "Father, forgive them, for they know not what they do." And they cast lots to divide his garments (Luke 23:34).

in my kingdom and sit on thrones judging the twelve tribes of Israel.

Jesus Foretells Peter's Denial

³¹"Simon, Simon, behold, Satan demanded to have you, that he might sift you like wheat, ³²but I have prayed for you that your faith may not fail. And when you have turned again, strengthen your brothers." ³³Peter said to him, "Lord, I am ready to go with you both to prison and to death." ³⁴Jesus said, "I tell you, Peter, the rooster will not crow this day, until you deny three times that you know me."

Scripture Must Be Fulfilled in Jesus

³⁵And he said to them, "When I sent you out with no moneybag or knapsack or sandals, did you lack anything?" They said, "Nothing." ³⁶He said to them, "But now let the one who has a moneybag take it, and likewise a knapsack. And let the one who has no sword sell his cloak and buy one. ³⁷For I tell you that this Scripture must be fulfilled in me: 'And he was numbered with the transgressors.' For what is written about me has its fulfillment." ³⁸And they said, "Look, Lord, here are two swords." And he said to them, "It is enough."

Jesus Prays on the Mount of Olives

³⁹And he came out and went, as was his custom, to the Mount of Olives, and the disciples followed him. ⁴⁰And when he came to the place, he said to them, "Pray that you may not enter into temptation." ⁴¹And he withdrew from them about a stone's throw, and knelt down and prayed, ⁴²saying, "Father, if you are willing, remove this cup from me. Nevertheless, not my will, but yours, be done." ⁴³And there appeared to him an angel from heaven, strengthening him. ⁴⁴And being in an agony he prayed more earnestly; and his sweat became like great drops of blood falling down to the ground. ⁴⁵And when he rose from prayer, he came to the disciples and found them sleeping for sorrow, ⁴⁶and he said to them, "Why are you sleeping? Rise and pray that you may not enter into temptation."

Betrayal and Arrest of Jesus

⁴⁷While he was still speaking, there came a crowd, and the man called Judas, one of the twelve, was leading them. He drew near to Jesus to kiss him, ⁴⁸but Jesus said to him, "Judas, would you betray the Son of Man with a kiss?" ⁴⁹And when those who were around him saw what would follow, they said, "Lord, shall we strike with the sword?" ⁵⁰And one of them struck the servant of the high priest and cut off his right ear. ⁵¹But Jesus said, "No more of this!" And he touched his ear and healed him. ⁵²Then Jesus said to the chief priests and officers of the temple and elders, who had come out against him, "Have you come out as against a robber, with swords and clubs? ⁵³When I was with you day after day in the temple, you did not lay hands on me. But this is your hour, and the power of darkness."

Peter Denies Jesus

⁵⁴Then they seized him and led him away, bringing him into the high priest's house, and Peter was following at a distance. ⁵⁵And when they had kindled a fire in the middle of the courtyard and sat down together, Peter sat down among them. ⁵⁶Then a servant girl, seeing him as he sat in the light and looking closely at him, said, "This man also was with him." ⁵⁷But he denied it, saying, "Woman, I do not know him." ⁵⁸And a little later someone else saw him and said, "You also are one of them." But Peter said, "Man, I am not." ⁵⁹And after an interval of about an hour still another insisted, saying, "Certainly this man also was with him, for he too is a Galilean." ⁶⁰But Peter said, "Man, I do not know what you are talking about." And immediately, while he was still speaking, the rooster crowed. ⁶¹And the Lord turned and looked at Peter. And Peter remembered the saying of the Lord, how he had said to him, "Before the rooster crows today, you will deny me three times." ⁶²And he went out and wept bitterly.

Jesus Is Mocked

⁶³Now the men who were holding Jesus in custody were mocking him as they beat him. ⁶⁴They also blindfolded him and kept asking him, "Prophesy! Who is it that struck you?" ⁶⁵And they said many other things against him, blaspheming him.

Jesus Before the Council

⁶⁶When day came, the assembly of the elders of the people gathered together, both chief priests and scribes. And they led him away to their council, and they said, ⁶⁷"If you are the Christ, tell us." But he said to them, "If I tell you, you will not believe, ⁶⁸and if I ask you, you will not answer. ⁶⁹But from now on the Son of Man shall be seated at the right hand of the power of God." ⁷⁰So they all said, "Are you the Son of God, then?" And he said to them, "You say that I am." ⁷¹Then they said, "What further testimony do we need? We have heard it ourselves from his own lips."

Betrayal is difficult to accept. Benedict Arnold betrayed his friend, George Washington, and his country during the Revolutionary War. As a result, many lives were lost. His name has been remembered in disgrace ever since. No matter how many good deeds he accomplished during his life, he will always be remembered as a traitor to his country.

But no betrayal was more disgraceful than the one committed by Judas Iscariot. Judas knew that the chief priests and the scribes wanted to put Jesus to death. He chose to help them by betraying his Master and his Friend. For a mere 30 pieces of silver (the price of a common slave), Judas agreed to "deliver him [Jesus] over to" the chief priests. (See Matt. 26:14–16.)

His opportunity came quickly. When Jesus and His disciples gathered in the upper room to share a Passover meal, Judas was with them. As the meal progressed, Jesus took the bread, broke it and gave it to them saying, "This is my body, which is given for you. Do this in remembrance of me" (Luke 22:19). Taking the cup of wine, after they had eaten, he said, "This cup that is poured for you is the new covenant in my blood." Yet in the midst of this most intimate moment, Jesus knew what was in Judas' heart. "But behold, the hand of him who betrays me is with me on the table" (22:21).

In a matter of hours, Judas led a band of soldiers along with the chief priests and other religious leaders to the place where they could do this deed with a minimum of witnesses—the Garden of Gethsemane.

But Judas was not the only betrayer. The religious leaders betrayed the Jewish people as well as Jesus by rejecting the One God sent as Savior and King. As Jesus observed, "Have you come out as against a robber, with swords and clubs? When I was with you day after day in the temple, you did not lay hands on me" (22:52–53). Their cowardly, jealous hearts caused them to betray the only Savior God was going to send.

All the disciples, in a sense, betrayed Jesus when they deserted Him. Peter, however, especially betrayed Jesus when he denied Him three times before the rooster crowed. Giving in to the fear of suffering the same fate as Jesus, he responded to a servant girl's accusation, "Woman, I do not know him" (22:57). Later, he declared

> ❝*We all fail Jesus at points in our lives. But the good news is that there's forgiveness.*❞

"Man, I am not." And an hour later, "Man, I do not know what you are talking about."

And even the Roman government betrayed Jesus. After an illegal trial before a hastily called assembly of the Jewish elders (22:66–71), Jesus was taken before Pilate. Pilate sent Him to Herod when he found out Jesus was from Galilee. After questioning Him briefly, Herod sent Jesus back to Pilate for final judgment. Pilate was a Roman. The Roman government was known to be merciless in their execution of justice, but they were usually fair. Pilate's decision was, "I did not find this man guilty of any of your charges against him" (23:14).

Despite that, Pilate caved in to the demands of the Jewish religious leaders. "He released the man who had been thrown into prison for insurrection and murder, for whom they asked, but he delivered Jesus over to their will" (23:25). Pilate betrayed Jesus as well as the Roman law which he was supposed to uphold. With this last hurdle cleared, the religious leaders had their way and Jesus was led off with two other criminals to be crucified.

But there is a bright spot in all this—and that is the forgiveness of Jesus. From the cross, in the midst of His agony, He said, "Father, forgive them, for they know not what they do" (23:34). To the thief on the cross beside Him, He extended not only forgiveness but a promise. "Truly, I say to you, today you will be with me in Paradise." (23:43). While the crowd was at its worst crying out, "Crucify, crucify him" (23:21), Jesus was at His best whispering, "Father, forgive them" (23:34).

After His Resurrection, Jesus would meet with Peter: the disciple who betrayed Him not once but three times. Yet Jesus forgave and gave him the responsibility to "feed my sheep" (John 21:17).

We all fail Jesus at points in our lives. Maybe you even feel you've betrayed Him. But the good news is that there's forgiveness. First John 1:9 says, "If we confess our sins, he is faithful and just to forgive us our sins and to cleanse us from all unrighteousness."

Jesus forgave those who nailed Him to the cross. Don't you think He can forgive you? Jesus forgave someone who was a thief and a murderer. Don't you think He can forgive you? Jesus forgave the one who publicly denied Him three times. Don't you think He can forgive you?

Turn to Him today, confess your sins, and let His forgiveness cleanse you from all you've done wrong. It's why He was born, why He lived, and why He died.

Go Deeper

Throughout His ministry, Jesus knew that He would eventually be killed. It was an appointment with a destiny planned before the foundations of the world. After Peter declared that Jesus was the Messiah (the One sent by God to die for our sins), Christ began to teach openly about it. He even announced that His death would be by crucifixion (John 12:32–33)—a lengthy, horrible form of execution.

Romans usually crucified a victim by first beating them with a whip with three lashes that had pieces of metal or bone tied at the ends. After the beating, the Roman soldiers made the person carry a heavy wooden crossbar to the place of crucifixion. Once there, soldiers tied or nailed the wrists of the victim to the wooden crossbar. They fastened the crossbar to an upright pole. They often nailed the victim's ankles to the pole, where he was left to suffer and die.

Why would the Son of God give up His rights and suffer this brutal death? Hebrews 12:2 says Jesus endured the cross in expectation of the joy that was set before Him. And the joy set before Him was this: that those who trust in Him might have their sins forgiven and receive eternal life.

Never forget. He did it for you.

Express It

Jesus suffered much and was willing to forgive. Is forgiveness hard for you? If there is someone who has hurt you or betrayed you and you find it hard to overcome that pain, their name likely comes to mind whenever the word forgiveness *is mentioned.*

Would you take a step toward forgiving that person today? First, realize what forgiveness means and what it doesn't mean. It doesn't mean that you condone the person's behavior; it does mean that you cease to feel resentful about the incident. Forgiveness means release. Ask Christ to help you release that person from the hurt they have caused you and to heal your heart. He'll do that for you.

Remember how much He has forgiven you and how willingly He has done it. That may make it easier to forgive someone who's hurt you.

Consider It

As you read Luke 22:1–23:56, consider these questions:

1) When Jesus arrived in Jerusalem, what was going on behind the scenes?

_____

_____

_____

2) What instructions did Jesus give when He sent Peter and John to prepare the Passover meal?

_____

_____

_____

3) Jesus knew He would be betrayed; what were the ultimate reasons?

_____

_____

_____

4) When the religious leaders gathered, what did they want to know? How did Jesus respond?

_____

_____

_____

5) Why did Herod want to see Jesus?

_____

_____

_____

6) What did the centurion who watched Jesus die decide about Him?

_____

_____

_____

7) Why do you think it's so hard for people to believe that Jesus is who He says? What made you believe Him?

_____

_____

_____

He Is Risen Indeed

Do you ever wonder if it's all true? Could it be that you've been misled and this stuff about Jesus is a myth? When thoughts like that occur, go back to the empty tomb. If it's true that Jesus was raised from the dead, then everything else is true as well.

Luke 24:1–53

The Resurrection

24 But on the first day of the week, at early dawn, they went to the tomb, taking the spices they had prepared. [2]And they found the stone rolled away from the tomb, [3]but when they went in they did not find the body of the Lord Jesus. [4]While they were perplexed about this, behold, two men stood by them in dazzling apparel. [5]And as they were frightened and bowed their faces to the ground, the men said to them, "Why do you seek the living among the dead? [6]He is not here, but has risen. Remember how he told you, while he was still in Galilee, [7]that the Son of Man must be delivered into the hands of sinful men and be crucified and on the third day rise." [8]And they remembered his words, [9]and returning from the tomb they told all these things to the eleven and to all the rest. [10]Now it was Mary Magdalene and Joanna and Mary the mother of James and the other women with them who told these things to the apostles, [11]but these words seemed to them an idle tale, and they did not believe them. [12]But Peter rose and ran to the tomb; stooping and looking in, he saw the linen cloths by themselves; and he went home marveling at what had happened.

On the Road to Emmaus

[13]That very day two of them were going to a village named Emmaus, about seven miles from Jerusalem, [14]and they were talking with each other about all these things that had happened. [15]While they were talking and discussing together, Jesus himself drew near and went with them. [16]But their eyes were kept from recognizing him. [17]And he said to them, "What is this conversation that you are holding with each other as you walk?" And they stood still, looking sad. [18]Then one of them, named Cleopas, answered

> # Key Verse
>
> *And as they were frightened and bowed their faces to the ground, the men said to them, "Why do you seek the living among the dead? He is not here, but has risen"*
> (Luke 24:5–6).

him, "Are you the only visitor to Jerusalem who does not know the things that have happened there in these days?" [19]And he said to them, "What things?" And they said to him, "Concerning Jesus of Nazareth, a man who was a prophet mighty in deed and word before God and all the people, [20]and how our chief priests and rulers delivered him up to be condemned to death, and crucified him. [21]But we had hoped that he was the one to redeem Israel. Yes, and besides all this, it is now the third day since these things happened. [22]Moreover, some women of our company amazed us. They were at the tomb early in the morning, [23]and when they did not find his body, they came back saying that they had even seen a vision of angels, who said that he was alive. [24]Some of those who were with us went to the tomb and found it just as the women had said, but him they did not see." [25]And he said to them, "O foolish ones, and slow of heart to believe all that the prophets have spoken! [26]Was it not necessary that the Christ should suffer these things and enter into his glory?" [27]And beginning with Moses and all the Prophets, he interpreted to them in all the Scriptures the things concerning himself.

²⁸So they drew near to the village to which they were going. He acted as if he were going farther, ²⁹but they urged him strongly, saying, "Stay with us, for it is toward evening and the day is now far spent." So he went in to stay with them. ³⁰When he was at table with them, he took the bread and blessed and broke it and gave it to them. ³¹And their eyes were opened, and they recognized him. And he vanished from their sight. ³²They said to each other, "Did not our hearts burn within us while he talked to us on the road, while he opened to us the Scriptures?" ³³And they rose that same hour and returned to Jerusalem. And they found the eleven and those who were with them gathered together, ³⁴saying, "The Lord has risen indeed, and has appeared to Simon!" ³⁵Then they told what had happened on the road, and how he was known to them in the breaking of the bread.

Jesus Appears to His Disciples

³⁶As they were talking about these things, Jesus himself stood among them, and said to them, "Peace to you!" ³⁷But they were startled and frightened and thought they saw a spirit. ³⁸And he said to them, "Why are you troubled, and why do doubts arise in your hearts? ³⁹See my hands and my feet, that it is I myself. Touch me, and see. For a spirit does not have flesh and bones as you see that I have." ⁴⁰And when he had said this, he showed them his hands and his feet. ⁴¹And while they still disbelieved for joy and were marveling, he said to them, "Have you anything here to eat?" ⁴²They gave him a piece of broiled fish, ⁴³and he took it and ate before them.

⁴⁴Then he said to them, "These are my words that I spoke to you while I was still with you, that everything written about me in the Law of Moses and the Prophets and the Psalms must be fulfilled." ⁴⁵Then he opened their minds to understand the Scriptures, ⁴⁶and said to them, "Thus it is written, that the Christ should suffer and on the third day rise from the dead, ⁴⁷and that repentance and forgiveness of sins should be proclaimed in his name to all nations, beginning from Jerusalem. ⁴⁸You are witnesses of these things. ⁴⁹And behold, I am sending the promise of my Father upon you. But stay in the city until you are clothed with power from on high."

The Ascension

⁵⁰Then he led them out as far as Bethany, and lifting up his hands he blessed them. ⁵¹While he blessed them, he parted from them and was carried up into heaven. ⁵²And they worshiped him and returned to Jerusalem with great joy, ⁵³and were continually in the temple blessing God.

I'm sure there are many special days in your life. The day you were born is pretty special. So is the day you graduated from school. What about the day you got married or the day your first child was born?

But one of the most special days in your life was a day that happened long before you were born. It was the day Jesus rose from the dead.

It all began on the first day of the week (Sunday). While different Gospel accounts focus on various aspects of the Resurrection, it is apparent that the tomb where they put Jesus' body was a busy place that morning. Sometime in the early hours of that day, Jesus, in physical form, left that tomb.

Later, perhaps hours, an angel descended from heaven and rolled back the stone from the mouth of the tomb (Matt. 28:2). His appearance was so overwhelming that the guards fell over like bowling pins.

Luke then tells us that toward dawn, a group of women arrived at the tomb. On the way they worried about how they would roll back the stone (Mark 16:3). When they got there, however, they found the problem taken care of—the stone was already rolled away. But then they discovered something that confused them even more—the body was gone.

While the women stood there puzzled, two men "in dazzling apparel" (obviously angels) appeared. They announced that Jesus had risen. Rushing back, the women told the disciples what had happened only to be met with unbelief. John tells us that he and Peter ran to the tomb and found it empty, but no angels were present.

Jesus Himself was busy. He met the group of women returning from the tomb and instructed them to tell the disciples to meet Him in Galilee (Matt. 28:10). He comforted a grieving Mary Magdalene (John 20:11–18). He took a stroll with two of His followers on the road to Emmaus (Luke 24:13–35). And, finally, on the evening of that day, He appeared to all the disciples but Thomas as they huddled behind locked doors for fear of the Jews (John 20:19–23).

Wow, what a day: empty tomb, terrifying angels, rolling boulders, fainting soldiers, unbelieving disciples, sobbing woman, and a three-

> *"When we wonder if all the things we've always believed are true, we can go back to the Resurrection."*

person Bible conference! That day stood out in the memory of all these people as one of the most significant days in their lives.

But what about you and me? What makes it one of the most significant days in our lives? Let's go back and see what the apostle Paul says about this day. In 1 Corinthians 15:16–17, he says, "For if the dead are not raised, not even Christ has been raised. And if Christ has not been raised, your faith is futile and you are still in your sins."

Paul points out that the Resurrection is the guarantee that our sins are paid for. On Calvary's cross, Jesus took upon Himself the sins of the whole world (1 John 2:2). If His sacrifice had not been enough to pay for those sins, He would have been trapped in death just as we are. His Resurrection, however, was God's confirmation that those sins were paid.

Furthermore, the Resurrection reminds us that we serve a Savior who is alive today just as He was 2,000 years ago. No other religion can say that. Muhammad is dead. Buddha is dead. All the great religious leaders of the past are dead. But not Jesus; Jesus is alive. We can talk to Him (prayer), and He talks to us (through His Word). He knows our trials and temptations and, through His Holy Spirit, is able to comfort and encourage us.

But remember this as well: Because Jesus was raised from the dead, you and I can know for sure that we will be raised from the dead. Jesus broke the power of death. The sin which once kept us in the grave has been paid for. We are freed not only from the penalty of sin but from the fear of death.

In addition, the Resurrection is the "proof positive" of our faith. When we wonder if all the things we've always believed are true, we can go back to the Resurrection. If the tomb wasn't empty, where was the body? Had there been a body, the religious leaders in Jerusalem would have been glad to bring it out to prove all this was nonsense. But if there was no body, if the tomb was truly empty, then everything else must be true as well.

While the day Jesus rose from the dead is special to all who were part of that event, it's also special to you and me. It changed our lives. The Resurrection made it possible for us to have a personal relationship with the living God. Our sins are forgiven, and we have the assurance of an eternity spent with our Savior in heaven.

Go Deeper

Jesus said: "For just as Jonah was three days and three nights in the belly of the great fish, so will the Son of Man be three days and three nights in the heart of the earth" (Matt. 12:40).

Some have claimed that if Jesus was crucified on Friday and rose on Sunday, He could not possibly be in the grave three days and three nights.

How do we explain this? Every attempt to explain the days and nights of Jesus' death both answers an objection and creates another. Some scholars take a figurative approach (i.e., Jesus didn't mean a literal three days and three nights but was using a figure of speech).

A better solution, however, is based on the Hebrew understanding of time. One of their rabbis said, "A day and a night are an *onah* (Hebrew term for a unit of time), and the portion of an *onah* is as the whole of it." Thus Friday counts as a "day and a night," Saturday counts as a "day and a night," and Sunday (since He was in the grave on part of that day) counts as a "day and a night." Those who believe Jesus was crucified on Wednesday can count three full days and three full nights. The problem is that a Wednesday crucifixion places Jesus in the grave four nights. A Thursday crucifixion doesn't answer the problem either. While we may not have an adequate explanation for the timing, what we know for sure is the truth. Jesus died, was buried, and three days later proved He was Lord even over death. Jesus is risen; He is risen indeed!

Express It

The Resurrection is a highly important event for you if you're a Christian. When you think about Christ's Resurrection, it's a time to celebrate His triumph over sin and death and therefore yours.

Draw a picture or import one (onto a computer document) that means "triumphant" to you. Then using markers, crayons, or WordArt, write words of rejoicing around your picture. Print or type your favorite scripture or an appropriate scripture verse under the picture.

Consider It

As you read Luke 24:1–53, consider these questions:

1) Who is the "they" in Luke 24:1? (See also 24:10.)

_____

_____

_____

2) What message did they receive when they arrived at the tomb?

_____

_____

_____

3) What did they do with this message?

_____

_____

_____

4) What are you doing with this message today?

_____

_____

_____

5) What did the two people on the road to Emmaus tell Jesus?

_____

_____

_____

6) How did Jesus respond?

_____

_____

_____

7) How did these people describe being with Jesus? What is your response when you've met with Jesus?

_____

_____

_____